LUZERNE AND LACKAWANNA COUNTIES
GHOSTS
Legends and Lore

by
Charles J. Adams III

Exeter House Books

LUZERNE AND LACKAWANNA COUNTIES GHOSTS, LEGENDS & LORE

©2007 Charles J. Adams III

For information contact:
EXETER HOUSE BOOKS
P.O. BOX 6411, Wyomissing, PA 19610
www.ExeterHouseBooks.com

ISBN: 978-1-880683-25-5
Printed in the United States of America

To Vera

TABLE OF CONTENTS

INTRODUCTION

I am credited as the author of this book, but in a large part, dozens of others have written it for me. They are those who lived the ghost stories you are about to read.

The folks in Northeast Pennsylvania are generally a genial, garrulous lot. The vast majority of those I contacted in the research phase of this book were more than willing to share their stories.

In the following pages, you will read about their experiences, often in their own words. No embellishment or amplification is necessary when the stories are presented in a forthright, firsthand, first-person fashion.

Sloshing in the wake of the writing of this book are the usual flotsam and jetsam residues of research–false leads, unanswered and/or unreturned telephone calls and emails; fully-researched stories purged at the last minute when the teller of the tale decided it was not in their best interest to allow their experiences to be published; and stories that surfaced just after the manuscript was shipped to the printer.

These represent the bane of the researcher and writer of books such as this. After 35 years of paranormal research and 25 books on the subject, however, I have become numb to such

1

disappointments.

Some readers may feel there is a disconnect between the contents of this volume and what they remember from their youth or have read on the Internet.

This era of unprecedented, instant, and anonymous communications has led to a soaring birth rate of new urban legends on the Internet.

In this book, you will not read about certain places in Luzerne and Lackawanna counties that have fallen into those ranks.

Details, however scant, about these and dozens of other "haunted" locations in the region are limited to those posted by online denizens who dwell in the nebulous nether regions of the web. Some of those stories may have merit, but others are placed in what I call my "they say" file. "They say" that *blah-blah-blah* is haunted by the ghost of *yada-yada-yada*. The "they" who said it is usually nowhere to be found.

In this book, you will read nothing about the house on Chase Street in West Pittston, a ghost fable that coursed its way in the mid-1980s through the local media into a book and then a movie. Ultimately, the entire matter was determined to be, well, less than credible.

You will read many stories that are pure folklore and/or legend, and others that could be considered legends in the making. This is the first book I have written that has been divided into three distinct sections: Ghosts, Legends, and Lore.

Many of those tales are admittedly quite tall, and many have been told and retold so often that they have morphed into myth. They still warrant yet another telling for yet another generation to consider.

Presenting ghost stories in a book is one thing. The written words flow from my fingers to the computer screen. They are then formatted into pages and books. They are but images of ink and paper.

Telling ghost stories eyeball-to-eyeball; watching those eyeballs widen and roll at the mention of grisly, ghoulish ghosts that may lurk right over the listeners' shoulders; and witnessing a collective shuddering as I speak of things that may go bump in the listeners' own nights-*that* is when and where stories of the dead come alive not only for the listeners, but for the teller.

I cannot watch those eyes as they read my books. I *can* watch, however, as they listen to my stories.

I like to tell ghost stories.

I like to scare people.

I have told ghost stories to gatherings of four and to groups of hundreds–and to folks aged four to one hundred. No matter where I go and to whom I relate the stories, the reactions are generally the same.

They like to hear ghost stories.

They like to be scared.

Indeed, from the "old school" oral tradition to the Internet, one thing has remained constant. People love to read ghost stories, hear ghost stories, and tell ghost stories.

I enjoy a good ghost story on film. Sadly, there are so few *good* ghost stories on film. I love to crack open a spellbinding ghost story book. And, I obviously relish writing ghost stories. But to me, the best ghost story is the one told or heard in a quiet, darkened room or on a crisp, autumn evening before the flickering glow of a crackling campfire.

But, the more I lamented the gradual decline and dousing of those campfire ghost stories, the more I realized that perhaps it hasn't declined at all.

That epiphany unfolded right before my eyes.

One dark and stormy night (it really was), I sat at my computer. The only light in the room was the glow of the computer monitor. The only sounds in that room were the clicking of my mouse and the ticking of the keys of the keyboard.

I was reading an email from a contributor to this book, and her words were chilling. I knew I was alone in the room, but got that sensation that someone was just over my shoulder, peering down at me. I wheeled around. Nothing. Nobody.

My eyes wearied by hours at the computer, I tried nonetheless to squint into the darkness and listen to the silence for signs that perhaps I was not alone.

I slumped back into my chair and took a deep breath. I was, I reckoned, quite alone. Alone, that is, except for the words on the screen and that glimmering glow of the monitor.

The words of the email–the *ghost story* of the email–had done their job.

Yes, perhaps many paranormal sites on the web can be mangled meshes of misinformation, but they they could also be considered as the heirs of a tradition established by the bards and shanachie of old.

Perhaps the Internet is really the world's largest haunted house, where stories and images may be explored by armchair ghost hunters on dark and stormy nights in gloomy, quiet rooms. Perhaps that computer monitor screen is nothing but an electronic campfire around which we gather to stimulate our imaginations.

Thanks for reading this book...
Charles J. Adams III

MORE BOOKS BY
CHARLES J. ADAMS III

Published by

EXETER HOUSE BOOKS

PO Box 4611, Wyomissing, PA 19610
www.ExeterHouseBooks.com

Coal Country Ghosts
Haunted Berks County
Tales from Baseballtown
Ghost Stories of Delaware County
Coal Country Ghosts, Legends, and Lore (Book One)
Atlantic County Ghost Stories
Ghost Stories of Chester County
Montgomery County Ghost Stories
Bucks County Ghost Stories
Philadelphia Ghost Stories
New York City Ghost Stories
Cape May Ghost Stories, Book I
Cape May Ghost Stories, Book II
Cape May Ghost Stories, Book III
Shipwrecks & Legends 'round Cape May
Pocono Ghosts, Legends & Lore, Book I
Pocono Ghosts, Legends & Lore, Book II
Ghost Stories of Pittsburgh & Allegheny Co.
Pennsylvania Dutch Country Ghosts
Ghost Stories of the Lehigh Valley
Ghost Stories of the Delaware Coast
Shipwrecks, Sea Stories and Legends of the Delaware Coast
Ghost Stories of Berks County, Book I
Ghost Stories of Berks County, Book II
Ghost Stories of Berks County, Book III
Berks the Bizarre
Legends of Long Beach Island
Shipwrecks Near Barnegat Inlet
Shipwrecks Off Ocean City (NJ)
Great Train Wrecks of Eastern Pennsylvania

*ALL TITLES MAY BE ORDERED ON-LINE OR AT MAJOR
BOOK STORES*

CARBONDALE'S
HAUNTED CITY HALL

I didn't have to venture far into Carbondale to find a ghost story. It was right there waiting for me at 1 Main Street, under the clock tower of the stately Romanesque Revival Carbondale City Hall.

Once inside the ca. 1892 landmark, I didn't

have to venture any farther for a ghost story than at the front desk of the Carbondale Police Department...the mayor's office...and the city clerk.

Actually, Mayor Justin M. Taylor was quick and cordial with his email response, but shunted me to the city clerk and the historical society for more information. "They both have worked in City Hall much longer than I have," the mayor said. "I've only been here three years, but I have heard some of the same types of [ghost] stories the police probably told you."

At the mayor's suggestion, my quest for the stories started with City Clerk Michele Bannon, who offered some thoughts on what could be the baseline for the hauntings.

"There are lots of theories," she said. "We do know that a city manager died in the mayor's office several decades ago. He died of a heart attack after a council meeting."

So, *he* is the ghost of city hall?

"And then," she continued, "there was once a jail down in the back of the building and there were a few deaths there, from hangings and other causes."

Aha! *They*, then, left their haunting marks?

"They also claim, and I don't know whether it's true or not, that there were deaths here when they were constructing the building."

The plot thickens.

"Oh yes, and then there was the horrible mine cave-in very near here. Fourteen miners died, and their bodies are still down there."

Very well, then. The choices are numerous.

Whatever imprinted the energies in the hallowed hall of Carbondale's government has made many workers there wary of certain areas of the building.

"At nighttime up here on the second floor," Bannon said, "you can often hear someone progressively walking through the halls. He can be heard walking on the old hardwood floors, one step at a time. And, nobody's up here at the time, of course."

Other incidents that have given certain employees at City Hall cause to believe it is haunted follow familiar paranormal patterns–items moving, icy chills, etc., etc.

The Carbondale Historical Society maintains its headquarters on the third floor of City Hall, and its executive director, Dr. S. Robert Powell, was quick to dismiss any ghost stories about the building.

"I do know that people seem to express a feeling about City Hall being haunted," he conceded, "but I cannot for the life of me imagine how it started."

A man of history, not mystery, Dr. Powell

took a pragmatic stance. "People seem to make these associations with big, old buildings that take on a kind of spooky quality in the popular mind. And then, it goes from there to their being haunted."

He did recall a contractor who was doing work in the building in the summer of 2006 who said he felt a presence in the room in which he was working. And, he has heard about certain city workers and police officers who don't want to venture above the second floor after dark.

"I sometimes wonder if they're not hearing me up here on the third floor," he laughed. "But, I'm very conspicuous, I don't sneak around, and I keep lights on, and I make a very clear presence."

Perhaps you do, Dr. Powell. But, perhaps another, usually less conspicuous being shares the space in which you tend your toils.

Detective Sergeant Jesse Van Deusen is a 15-year veteran of the Carbondale Police Department. And although his encounter with the entity on the upper floors of City Hall took place when he was a rookie patrolman, he still finds it difficult to detail what happened one frigid night in March, 1993.

He had just completed pulling a double shift and was facing a day in court the next day, a Monday. He received permission to find a cozy, warm place and take a nap in the wee, small hours of that Monday morning.

The most enticing spot to take a nap was a comfy couch on the second floor.

"I had heard the stories about people seeing ghosts up there," Sgt. Van Deusen said, "but we'd just joke about it." Besides, the sergeant was tired.

He took off his gunboat downstairs, grabbed a flashlight and portable radio, and headed upstairs for some precious shuteye. As he started up the steps, one of his colleagues joked, "Hey, be careful the ghost doesn't get you!" The weary patrolman dismissed it as so much small talk.

It was four in the morning. He remembered that because the numbers of a clock on a table near the second floor couch had just clicked over to 4:00.

He would snuggle up with his long, heavy, fur-collared reefer jacket as a makeshift blanket. He settled in and pulled the furry collar over his eyes while clutching the radio against his chest.

"All of a sudden," he remembered, "I felt very, very, *very*, wicked cold. And, I felt as if someone was standing over me, looking down at me.

"Initially, of course, I thought it might have been one of the guys from downstairs." But, he knew better.

"As I was lying there," he continued, "I felt as if there was somebody an inch away from my face, staring at me.

"I tried to open my eyes, but I didn't. I don't know if I was afraid to, or I couldn't.

"The next thing I felt, as God is my witness, was something pulling on my pant leg. It picked my leg up about a foot off the couch. Mind you, my leg was tucked under the long jacket. But it picked my leg up and pulled it straight out!"

He said he still felt the icy chill and the overbearing sensation that someone was standing over him, and then–"I felt my leg being pulled out, and then dropped!"

All the while, he tried to push the button of the radio, but couldn't.

And then, the "wicked cold" sensation lifted.

"I don't mind saying I was scared as hell," he said.

He gathered his senses, flung his coat off, and ran toward the staircase. "I leaped probably 15 steps to the landing and another bunch of steps to the first floor. I ran to the back of the police station and I stopped. One of the cops who's retired now looked at me and asked 'What the **** happened to you?'

"Well, I was as white as a piece of paper! And, I looked at the clock that was on top of the TV and it said 4:11. So, I was only up there for 11 minutes."

For the next three hours–until 7 a.m. that Monday morning, Van Deusen sat downstairs, head in hand. "The last thing I ever would have done was tell anybody about what happened up there," he said. "After all, I was one of the guys who joked around about those who said they believed there were ghosts up there."

As best as he could, he tried to rationalize what happened. He could not. "All I know," he sighed, "is that something picked my leg up."

To this day, Sgt. Van Deusen will not go on the second floor after dark.

Does he think Carbondale's City Hall is haunted? He answered with one word: "Yes."

The irony of all of this is that he was one of those who mocked others who had told stories of their experiences on the upper floors of the building and their hesitance to go there alone, or at night.

Other police officers–each rugged veterans of the force–also said they would just as soon not venture upstairs after dark.

Neither they, nor Sgt. Van Deusen, nor the city clerk, nor the city historian, nor anyone else is likely to ever identify and quantify the spirit activity in the building, but there seems to be little doubt that someone–or something–haunts that fine, old structure.

CLIFFORD'S HAUNTED HOTEL

The Internet is a worldwide electronic bulletin board where meaningful messages may be posted and invaluable resources are available.

However, it can also be a deep, dark pit of exploitation where misinformation and myths run wild. It can be a breeding ground for urban legends and an incubator of demagoguery and deception.

This "information superhighway," as it was described in its infancy does indeed serve as a conduit of credible communications. But, for every legitimate, meaningful, and monitored paranormal web sites there are a dozen that wallow in the gutters of that "highway."

Imaginative graphics and impressive names notwithstanding, too many of those sites are nothing but supernatural circus side shows.

The serious researcher of ghost stories and haunted places must exercise extreme caution and discretion. It is all too easy to besmirch or destroy the reputation of a business or institution with the indiscriminate, sometimes intentionally malicious labeling of a place as "haunted" or "hexed."

It is likewise convenient for the aspiring ghost hunter or *ad hoc* paranormal research organization to be led astray by the misguided missives that are placed on the web and perpetuate the irresponsible and reckless postings of these would-be authorities.

Case in point: The Clifford Hotel.

On the extreme northern fringe of "Coal Country," is the crossroads village of Clifford. Where those roads cross is the Clifford Hotel.

I tend to be quite provincial in the titling and publishing of these books, and when I noticed that Clifford was *just* over the Lackawanna line and in Susquehanna County, my first thoughts were to ignore what I had heard about the Clifford Hotel and save it should I ever do a book about hauntings in Susquehanna County.

As that is not likely, I decided to look into the alleged activity in the Clifford Hotel. That activity was just too tempting to ignore:

"Clifford, PA: The Clifford Hotel:
"It is said there are over 30 spirits haunting this place. There are voices heard
in the main lobby of men, women,
and children that were brutally murdered by
a man who went insane in the hotel.
"Upstairs there is a very hostile man who doesn't like anyone to go on that floor and will do anything to keep everyone off that floor. There have been sightings on certain nights that the hotel will be fully light up (sic) *and there will be music coming from it.*

16

*"It is watched by the police heavily
and there is NO TRESPASSING!"*

Very well! It sounded like a perfect candidate for the pages of this book.

But, those words were taken from entries in web sites that purport to serve as directories of haunted places. I learned many years ago to not trust these entries and research anything myself.

I have been victimized by the idle ramblings of amateur researchers who have totally misinterpreted and/or misrepresented information in one of my books and slapped it on the internet. I could cite several examples of stories I "broke" being totally and thoroughly expanded and exaggerated on the Internet.

You just read the description of the haunted Clifford Hotel. And, before I go any further, yes...the Clifford Hotel is haunted. But by whom, and by how many ghosts? Let us find out from the primary sources.

I was apprised of the Clifford Hotel's ghosts by a police officer in Carbondale who showed me the entry on his computer. I asked him if he knew about the hotel, and he said he did. He also said he wondered where the author of the blurb got his information. He wondered why the *"It is watched by the police heavily and there is NO TRESPASSING!"* line was there, as he was certain the hotel was not vacant–it was occupied, and still in business.

So, to Clifford I went, in search of answers and, hopefully, a story about those "30 spirits" and the ghost of that "hostile man" on an upper floor.

"When I read that on the Internet," said a surprised Ted Wells, "I thought they were talking about some other Clifford Hotel."

There is no other Clifford Hotel, as far as my research could determine and as far as Ted Wells was concerned.

And, he should know. Ted has owned the

The Clifford Hotel

Clifford Hotel for 17 years and is proud and protective of its history.

Built in 1877, the Clifford Hotel had gone

through only a handful of other owners before Ted took over. And, he has a vested interest in not only the history, but the haunting of the hotel. You see, he lives on the second floor of the hotel. "I hope I'm not the crazy guy they're talking about," he quipped.

He did confirm that there have been incidents in the hotel, on each of the floors, that could be interpreted as "supernatural" in nature. And, an impromptu barside exchange between a pair of faithful patrons, a bartender, and Ted Wells revealed that several regulars and workers, on several occasions, have experienced events that have led them to believe that a ghost or two–but probably not 30–stroll the rustic floors of the hotel.

"The back door has opened and closed by itself many times," Ted Wells said. "Upstairs, on the third floor, there are always unexplained noises. We had a fire up there that gutted the third floor. But still, those same sounds can be heard. Apparently the fire didn't chase the spooks away!"

No, Ted, it did not.

An independent "sensitive" individual visited the Clifford Hotel with no knowledge of the hysterical information that had been written on the web. His task was to read the Clifford Hotel and determine whether it harbored any spirit energies.

Not two steps into the hotel, on the barroom

(right) side, the residual spirit of a very strong-minded male was encountered. It seems to be protective, on guard, and vigilant.

A name was suggested in the psychic reading: Melvin.

Not only did the visitor not know of the 30 ghosts, the murder victims, or the crazy man; he also was not told the names of the previous owners.

The owner of the hotel from 1934 to 1958: Melvern Spedding.

Melvin/Melvern? Could it be that his spirit remains at the front door, protective, on guard, and vigilant?

Although the energy was encountered on the main floor and inside the building, the visiting reader urged employees to keep an eye on the front porch swing, as it may move–seemingly on its own, but actually because of Melvin, or Melvern's fairly powerful presence.

There are other spirits in the Clifford Hotel, according to the casual but conclusive reading. Another ethereal energy seems to have the run of the place, according to the sensitive. As the ghostly flow of energy is not impeded by walls, it is likewise not contained by floors. The second ghost in the Clifford Hotel was described as young, but very wizened to the ways of the world.

She could have been a cleaning lady, or a

woman who, to be kind, provided comfort to male guests. It was felt that her death there was sudden and possibly violent. The energy was interpreted as sorrowful and confused.

Her ghost could best be seen or sensed on the first floor, crossing as a gentle, cool breeze diagonally from the bar through the dining room and to the back door that Ted Wells said has been known to open on its own.

Perhaps it is not opening "on its own," but with a little help from the forlorn phantom that sweeps through the first floor from time to time.

There are other entities within the walls of the Clifford Hotel, but they swirl in a veritable stew of supernatural energy, none with a strong enough identity to be singled out like the man and the girl.

When asked if there could indeed be as many as 30 ghosts in the hotel, the reader of its energies shrugged and indicated that anything is possible, but that number, for a hotel that size, is a bit unrealistic.

The Green Fox of Gibson Street

Some people harbor horror stories that are rooted in their childhood. Perhaps that mythical monster that lurked under the bed or in the closet remains embedded so deeply in their minds and memories that it surfaces as a phobia or fear throughout their lives.

Some adults still hold within them the secrets of childhood such as an imaginary playmate.

Christine Yarns Schaefer will never forget the mysterious green fox of her childhood in a house that once stood on Gibson Street in Scranton.

It is likely that she will never know what it was, what it represented, or indeed if it was real or imagined.

It is also likely that it was not imagined, as

she recalled and related her childhood experiences.

"In 1947," Christine said, "my parents were forced to move. The house they were renting on Meade Avenue was sold. World War II had ended and that left a housing shortage in the area. We moved to a second floor apartment on East Gibson Street in Scranton. Those type of apartments were called cold water flats. The second story apartment was heated by a pail a day in the front room and a cold/gas combination in the kitchen.

"The house had been a one family home but was converted into a two family up and down. My bedroom faced the railroad bridge. I could sit in my bed and watch trains as they passed by.

"In this little bedroom was a small bathroom, the only bathroom in this cold water flat apartment. It had a toilet and a chain pull light. There was a strange wall in this bathroom that seem to do nothing. It was not a outside wall. It was just there.

"The bathroom was always cold, even in the heat of summer. There were no windows in the bathroom.

"My mother wanted a place to store towels and blankets. She asked my father to make her a closet in the bathroom. My father removed the wall that seem to do nothing. This strange wall was full of dirt in the center.

"The dirt in the wall was taken away. There

was a outside wall behind this false wall. My father built my mother her towel/blanket closet."

Christine said she and her family were particularly vexed by a door that simply would not stay shut.

"At first my parents believe the reason the door would not stay closed was because of the trains. The house shook when the trains went by."

But, the restless door became an innocent nuisance compared with what appeared in her bedroom.

"In the fall of 1950," she continued, "a brilliant green fox appeared in my bedroom. My mother called the priest (Russian Orthodox) to come and bless the house."

The blessing may have taken effect on other matters in the house, but Christine's menacing intruder continued to visit.

"The green fox still appeared each evening," she said. "It would sit on a day bed that was in the room near the window. As the spirit appeared on a regular basis, it grew larger."

Note the sudden transition from "green fox" to "spirit." In the more than a half-century that has passed since the creature came into her life, she still has no answers.

"I have been asked if it had the body of a fox. I do not remember.

"It was a brilliant green fox to me. Years

later when my mother could talk about the green fox, she told me it looked like it had the head of a fox but the body of a child."

As bizarre as that may have seemed, Christine said the phantom was never really threatening.

"It never did anything to us as a family," she recalled. "It would just sit and look at us and grin. It never made a sound. After a while, the green fox even started to appear in the daytime.

"It appeared one evening when my father was home, he shut the door to my bedroom. My father was not a believer in ghosts or spirits but we would move out of that place in less than a year."

Christine said the fox, or spirit, or whatever it was, only appeared to members of her family. And, it did not seem to follow them to their new house. Her parents told her they believed it was trapped in that little room in the East Gibson Street house.

She has since moved from Scranton, but returned to find that the house had been demolished. Only the stone front steps were visible.

Despite the presence of that vacant lot, Christine's memories were anything but empty.

"My family would never talk about the evil that seem to be in that room of that house," she said. What did I and my family see? I will never know. But in all these years I have never forgotten the bright green color. The Green Fox was real to me. It happened too many times to be just a legend in our family."

Then again, Christine isn't really sure what that green beast might have been.

"I do not think the green fox was a ghost," she ventured, "but then again I was a kid, and who really knows?

It is obvious that the unsolved mystery has left an indelible mark on her life. "I would have loved if the house was still standing," she lamented. "I would gone over to see if it would appear again. I would have lots of questions. I believe it wanted something."

But, what it was and what it wanted will forever remain as unanswered questions.

Unless, that is, something new is built on the site of Christine's old home and the Green Fox of Gibson Street once again goes on the prowl.

THE LADY IN WHITE
...and other Courthouse Ghosts

The Lackawanna County Courthouse is a symbol of both the county, the city of Scranton, and–as the site of hearings of President Theodore Roosevelt's Anthracite Coal Strike Commission in 1902–American labor history.

The building stands on land that was once so soggy it was called the "Lily Pond" and used for ice skating before it was donated by the Lackawanna Iron and Coal Co. to the newly-formed county in 1881.

To shore up the soil to support the building, tunnels were built from the iron furnaces. Mine cars carried dirt and slag through the tunnels to the construction site.

The 4.7-acre square that wraps around the building once housed the county's gallows, where condemned criminals met their maker at the end of a rope.

A stalwart structure and imposing edifice, the Victorian Gothic courthouse looks like it should be–and indeed *is*–haunted.

Reports of lights turning themselves on in unoccupied offices, the steady and unmistakable footfall of phantoms in corridors, and the overlying sensation that unseen entities are always somewhere nearby have led some night workers to believe, without any doubt in their minds, that the building is populated by at least two ghosts.

One is the so-called "Lady in White," whose name should be an indicator of her countenance. Who she is (or was), nobody knows. What they do know is that for decades, her faint image has been seen tangentially by several employees on the second floor of the building. One member of the cleaning crew said he actually saw the "Lady" sail silently over his head on the second floor.

Another spirit is that of a pale male who frequents the first floor. Again, there is no indication as to his identity.

A court administration employee claimed he saw a mysterious couple on the first floor while he was moving office equipment. It was a weekend, and nobody should have been where he had seen them. When he attempted to get a better visual fix on them, they had disappeared.

Stories about unexplainable aromas, sights, sounds, and wild temperature fluctuations have been bandied about for many years and on levels ranging from county judges to the cleaning crew.

The official view of it all is that it's an old, creaky building that is bound to have its sensory quirks. A county spokesperson contacted for a comment on reports that the courthouse dismissed any notion of ghosts there. Every one of those sights, sounds, smells, and sensations probably has a rational, natural explanation, they maintained.

The operative word there would be...*probably*. Try telling that to the next person who watches as the Lady in White glides across a second floor hallway.

The Hell Dog

The story is told by one of the pillars of the community in Luzerne County.

"Because of where I work and what I do," he said, "I would prefer that my name not be mentioned in the story. But I would swear in any court or church that what I will tell you is the absolute truth."

Throughout this book are other stories told with the guarantee of anonymity. While I realize that some readers may be suspicious of the credibility of such stories, they will have to trust the author that every word has come from reliable sources who–for whatever reasons–have asked that their names not be used. It is a professional courtesy extended from the story writer to the story teller.

Having said that, let us proceed with the man's harrowing story of an encounter he had in a fine home on the outskirts of Freeland.

"I freely admit that I have always been a fan of stories of the paranormal, with Edgar Allan Poe among my favorite authors. But, never in my life did I dream I'd actually live in such a kind of story.

"It all started when my wife and I bought our property in 1996. It was exactly what we had been looking for, and seemed so perfect in every respect. We knew that the previous owners had both gone into a nursing home and died, and their children wanted nothing of the property. But, we didn't ask a lot of questions because we thought the deal might fall through if were too inquisitive.

"Well, we bought it and settled in quickly. From the get-go, it felt like home–exactly where we should be.

"But one day, something really strange

31

777

happened. My wife and I were both outside on a back patio area planting flowers and doing odd yard work. It was a nice spring day.

"Every once in a while, I noticed that she seemed distracted by something in the far corner of the yard. It's a big yard, and that corner is about 100 feet away. I just noticed that she would occasionally stop her work and glance that way. It was no big deal and I didn't say anything. But quietly, I thought something was going on. Maybe she just saw a squirrel or something. In any case, I didn't approach her about it.

"Well, life went on. We made some changes in what we call the 'inner yard' and planned more changes on the outer parts of the property. One day I was taking a walk around the perimeter of the yard and reached the corner my wife had been glancing at. Now, that part of the yard has no fence. The grass of the yard simply abuts a farm field that surrounds it.

"As I was looking around out there, trying to figure out where I might put a fence and maybe a small truck patch garden, I heard a growling sound. It's wide open out there, no trees, no high bushes. So, I figured that whatever was growling would be visible. The sound seemed to come from just a few feet away. Naturally, I looked around, figuring a dog was close by. But even when I looked directly at where I had heard the sound, I saw nothing.

"I swear to you that I heard the growling just as if there was a dog–what sounded like a very large dog–within a couple feet of me. It was not my imagination, and that growling sound went on for maybe five minutes. It wasn't echoing or anything like that. It was the sound of a dog growling very near me...a dog that wasn't there."

The gentleman shook his head and took a breath as he continued his story. He said he'd just stop talking if his story seemed too unbelievable. But, he was urged to go on.

"Well, I lived with this for a couple of days until one night my wife and I were talking about the improvements we were hoping to make in the yard. Then, she dropped the blockbuster on me.

"When I mentioned something about putting a fence and garden out in that far corner, she perked up. I could tell that I hit a sour note with her. Now, I had almost forgotten about the day I caught her looking out in the yard for no apparent reason. But, that growling incident was still bugging me.

"So, when I talked about the fence and that corner, she shook her head 'no.' Then, she came right out and said 'I don't think we should do anything in that corner. It scares me.'

"I was, of course, a little shocked. But, I also felt that we were coming to some sort of a confession time. Then, she told me that on several occasions, she had been in the 'outer yard' and had heard–get this–a growling sound, as if a large dog was there.

"You can probably figure out the rest. She told me about her experiences and I told her about mine. We were both stunned that neither of us had told the other the first time it happened. But, of course, both of us thought the other one would think we were crazy if we said anything then.

"Now that it was out in the open, we talked about what it might have really been. The absolute only conclusion we could both come up with is that it was the growling of a distant animal that somehow could be heard in that corner of the yard."

Both husband and wife, however, also conceded that what they had heard was there, in that corner, not filtering in from afar.

Although they both believed nothing would come of it, they agreed to try to find an explanation.

"All of a sudden," the man continued, "I had a feeling that I really was in the midst of a story that would at least be classified as 'unexplained,' if not 'paranormal.' Little did I know what was to come.

"Although my wife thought we should keep it to ourselves, I mentioned the incident to our nearest neighbor. I treated it as if we were both kooks and imagined the growling sound. I tried to downplay it until they took it to another level.

"We were both shook up a little when that neighbor told us that maybe it was best we didn't do much in that corner of the yard. Of course, we asked why.

"He told us that the previous owners of our house had used that corner as a private pet cemetery. To his knowledge, at least three of their dogs had been buried out there. His wife said there might have been more.

"They said that the former owners were a little off-center, and they were convinced that one of the dogs, a large mixed breed, might actually have been buried alive! As crazy as that seemed, the woman said she recalled that the dog had gone into fits of some kind and was literally beaten to a pulp with a shovel by the man who used to live in our house. Both of our neighbors believed that the dog might have been just barely alive when they buried it in a deep hole back in that corner of the yard.

"They said that they, too, had heard a growling sound–the exact sound that dog would make when it was alive–back in that corner where their yard meets ours. They are sensible people and knew that the sound wasn't coming from inside the soil. But, they were firmly convinced that the growling ghost of that dog remains out there.

"They called it 'The Hell Dog,' and when

they mentioned that phrase it gave me the willies. Again, I have no problems watching horror movies or reading ghost stories, but the notion of having a ghostly dog in our own yard was more than a little nerve-wracking."

He said the neighbors had not only heard the ghostly growling but claimed to have seen a low, shadowy form lurking in that section of the yard. "That," the man said, "was nearly enough for my wife to want to move out. But we both agreed that the house and yard were too much to our liking to let a ghost, and certainly not a ghost *dog* run us out.

"Maybe it was influenced by my neighbor's story, but I swear that I have also seen that shadowy figure out there. Early in the morning and just before sunset I have looked out there and have seen something. And, neither my wife nor I go anywhere near that corner any more. Neither of us have heard the growling sound lately. We moved some large rocks there to separate the yard from that corner. We figure that if it is a graveyard–even a dog graveyard–it deserves respect. We have just let it become overgrown with ground cover.

"Maybe that will let the Hell Dog rest in peace."

The Bagunk

Loch Ness has its Monster. Tibet has its Yeti. New Jersey has its Devil.

Newport Township, Luzerne County has its Bagunk.

Among the first places a researcher of local legends, lore, and haunts visits in any particular community are the police stations and post offices.

If a property is haunted, or said to be haunted, it is likely the local mail carriers or police officers will know about it. Whether they share their knowledge with the researcher is another story. But, when I entered the post office in Glen Lyon with the simple question, "Do you know of any haunted places around town?" Postmaster Jeffrey A. Stanton was all ears.

Without a blink, he answered: "Well, you know about the Bagunk, don't you?"

Without a blink, I answered: "Uh, no, I do not!"

He hastened to the back room of the vest-pocket postal facility and emerged seconds later with a clipping from the Times-Leader that told the tale of the township's elusive, legendary creature.

That story centered on the St. Michael's and

St. Andrew's cemeteries along the Main Road at the west end of Glen Lyon.

From one of those graveyards–and no one knows for sure which one–rises the spirit that has somehow taken on the name of The Bagunk.

Armed with the newspaper clippings, I thanked the postmaster and left the post office. As I was returning to my car, I asked an elderly gent who was entering the the post office if, by any chance, he had ever heard of the legend.

"It's not a legend," he shot back. "I seen it many times."

"Seen what?" I asked him.

"The Bagunk," he answered. "The ghost or whatever it is that hangs around St. Michael's cemetery."

By his demeanor, I knew he was not in the mood to trivialize the story.

"When I was a kid," he continued, "our parents told us to stay out of the cemeteries out there because of the monster. Well, that was just to try to keep us in line. And, naturally, them telling us to stay out meant we wanted to go there even more. So, one night five of us kids–we were about 15–went up there. It wasn't late at night, but it was getting dark.

"We weren't a bunch of crazy kids looking for cheap thrills. We were really interested in trying to see The Bagunk, if it was real, and whatever it was. One of the guys, and he's gone now, went on to become a history teacher.

"Well, we were prowling around the graveyard, hoping something would happen but knowing nothing probably would. Then, all of a sudden, we heard a rustling of leaves and the swoosh of a breeze. Well, that could have been anything. But it was The Bagunk, I'll tell you!"

The man, who didn't give me his name and said I should just call him an "old coot from Wanamie," was quite serious about his story. "I really haven't told the story to too many people," he said, "because they'd think it was just some nutty story from an overactive imagination."

"Even back then," he continued, "we knew the difference between mine fog, swamp gas, and that kind of stuff. What we saw in the cemetery was none of that.

"What we saw was a ghost, plain and simple. Call it The Bagunk or a spook, or whatever, but it was there, plain as could be.

"When we heard that sound of wind, we all looked over toward a tree line and saw a cloudy figure gliding just over the grass. It had the rough shape of a human being, but didn't make any motions. It just glided over the top of the grass and *through* a couple of tombstones. It acted like it had no idea we were there, and didn't much care if we were.

"All of that lasted maybe ten seconds, but the five us huddled together like wimps. We all stood there dead silent. It took a few seconds after the thing disappeared that we loosened up and started talking about it."

So, what was "the thing?" Was it a ghost, a monster, or a trick?

"I will tell you right now that it was not a trick," the man shot back. "There's no way. And, it wasn't a monster. It was a ghost, plain and simple. Plain and simple."

He said it could have been what has prompted stories of The Bagunk over the years. Most folks in Newport Township seem to believe The Bagunk is a composite of many experiences by many people over many years in the cemeteries.

Many Bagunk accounts, some far more vivid than that of the "old coot," have circulated. Many of them have been immediately discounted as pure folklore.

As for a baseline, or origin of the story, some say it all goes back to the untimely, accidental death of a young man near the cemeteries in the 1970s.

The "old coot" didn't believe that. "What we saw," he said, "we saw long before then. I don't know what it is or who it was. I just know there's something up there."

❦

HAUNTED HALLS OF HIGHER EDUCATION

Kirby Hall

Imposing and impressive as it stands in command of the corner of South and South River streets, Kirby Hall represents the very best of the very fine institution that is Wilkes University.

Since the elegant Victorian Gothic mansion was given to Wilkes University (then Bucknell

41

University Junior College) in 1941, it has served the school in many capacities. And, in the more than 65 years it was a private residence, it accumulated many tales.

Built by Stephen Leonard Thurlow, the building acquired its present name from Fred Morgan Kirby, who purchased it in 1905. Kirby, whose Wilkes-Barre retail business evolved into the F.W. Woolworth Company, made many renovations to his spacious home in the 35 years he lived there. Upon his passing in 1940, his son Allan donated it to the college.

Those tales that building could tell are tucked deep within its thick stone walls. But on occasion the players in those tales come to call in the form of ghostly activities that have provided many unsettling experiences for many unsuspecting students and staff members for many years.

Dr. Harold E. Cox, a gentleman who has been on the Wilkes University campus for 44 years, holds much of that history within him and within the pages of the books he has written and published about the school and the legendary street car systems of Luzerne and Lackawanna counties.

"I did about 75 books," he said through an ever-present smile and with a dignified drawl that still shines through from his Virginia upbringing.

"I published a book in 2006," he said. "But I

think that'll be the last of the street car books," he added with a chuckle, "because my audience is all dead!"

When it came to the dead–as in ghosts, and as in ghosts on the Wilkes campus–his smile widened. He riffled through dusty volumes on his cluttered shelf and pulled out a picture of the late, lamented Conyngham Mansion that was a magnificent campus structure until it burned to the ground right before Christmas, 1968. "It was definitely an 'Addams Family' style mansion," the retired head of the History Department said. "It was one of the most ornate buildings in town. There were stories told about that place."

But, what of the stories of Kirby Hall, Dr. Cox?

"Well, the Kirby house is an interesting structure. From the beginning it seemed to have problems. There was a man killed in the pool parlor–the billiards room–I believe at the time the Thurlows lived there. I have never been able to pin that down, exactly, though."

Legend has it that the murder victim was a shiftless character with the unlikely name of Poker Pan. William V. Lewis made reference to the alleged murder in a paper about the building and placed the crime sometime around the turn of the 20th century. He said the killing was over "a gambling dispute."

Dr. Cox said it would take extensive digging in newspaper morgues (which he has done), but even that may not yield the story. "I would assume that a murder in the home of an outstanding citizen would have attracted attention," he speculated, "unless they had enough power to surpress it."

While there is no firm baseline to the haunting of Kirby Hall, there are certainly many accounts of encounters with the resident wraiths there.

Several individuals have reported strange sounds and sights in the building by day and night, for several years.

Dr. Cox has attempted to trace many of those phenomena to natural, not supernatural roots. "I'm very skeptical about ghost stories," he said. "If I can't see it, feel it, eat it, or kick it in the (butt), I don't believe in it. I'm a cynic."

Dr. Bonnie Culver, associate professor of English and director of the Master of Arts in Creative Writing program at Wilkes, isn't quite as suspicious.

"I'm probably more of an agnostic about it," she said. "I had some experiences with folks who had been close to me and who had passed away, but I dismissed that as wishful thinking–wanting to see that person again.

"I didn't feel that I wasn't open to it," she continued, "but I didn't feel that it was something

I was looking for."

Looking for it or not, Bonnie found it at Kirby Hall–*it* being an experience she will never forget.

"I was teaching a night class on the third floor of the Kirby when there were classrooms up there," she said. "I stayed behind with a couple of students, and then they left."

Dr. Culver was in the process of descending the three levels of steps that course through the open staircase of the building when it happened.

"As I turned and started to enter the lobby area on the second floor," she continued, "I thought I saw a shadow.

"I stopped and thought it was a student who had just left. I called out her name and when I did, the shadow intensified and it became the shadowy figure of a woman."

The figure was drifting past windows in the dim landing below her.

"It turned and started coming up the stairs toward me. I felt immediate fright," she said with a nervous laugh. "The hair on the back of my neck stood up, I felt a chill...the whole thing. I had enough. I went out the side door and down the back stairs."

Bonnie composed herself and in the light of the next day assessed the situation in an attempt to find a rational explanation for what had happened the previous night. She went to the spot where she was standing and looked down to where the shadow had morphed into a human female form.

"I looked at the sconces on the wall," she said, "where the waistline of the shadow had been. Those sconces are about eight feet high over the floor!"

However she tried to explain her experience away, she could not. And, a later comment from colleague Dr. Darin Fields further convinced Bonnie that Kirby is a haunted Hall.

"Dr. Fields was teaching a night class and was coming back from the library toward Kirby Hall," she recalled. "He looked up and swore he saw me sitting in the window seat.

"He decided to go up the back stairs and scare me, just for the fun of it. But, as soon as he turned the corner he felt the same kind of cold and hair-raising that I had described. He turned around, hustled back down the stairs, and left!"

Dr. Fields, the Dean of the College of Arts, Humanities and Social Sciences at Wilkes, was miffed by the vision. "Whatever he saw up there," Bonnie Culver said, "could not have been me. I was up in Binghamton, New York, at that time."

So, did Dr. Culver's encounter in Kirby Hall alter her belief in ghosts? "I definitely think there's something there," she said, "because I have had a couple other experiences since then."

That Kirby Hall is haunted is well known throughout Wilkes. Over the years, several maintenance workers have refused to go into its basement by themselves. These are fairly rough, tough guys who fear little–except ghosts.

One of the only remainders from the earliest years of the mansion is an ornate grandfather's clock whose pendulum has a penchant for stopping. It is said that several maintenance workers who have attempted to fix the clock have recoiled from it when a strange, foreboding energy emanated from the timepiece.

Students have circulated their own stories about the Kirby Hall ghosts for many years. Their sightings have included an elegantly-attired woman on the staircase and a shifty-eyed, small man in the old music room. Their sounds range from a cackling laughter that can rise almost everywhere throughout the old mansion to a moaning, sobbing female whose sad sighs can be heard faintly echoing at the base of the staircase.

Others have had experiences in other buildings on the Wilkes University campus.

Bedford Hall shares a few traits with Kirby Hall. Each is a handsome Victorian Gothic 19th century former residence, each *looks like* it should be haunted, and according to reports, each *is* haunted.

The Bedford Hall stories are a bit more

elusive than those at Kirby. However, one Wilkes employee who wished to remain anonymous ("If you use my name in a book, they'd think I'm nuts and fire me," he said) believes the ghost is a young man who is bound to remain trapped in the building as punishment for a sin he committed there.

"All I know," the informant said, "is that Bedford can be downright spooky. A couple of us have caught quick glimpses of a guy wearing an old-fashioned suit, looking like one of those gangsters in an old movie. None of us ever saw a face, just that cheesy suit and a hat. No sooner do we see him, he vanishes. I'll tell you, it's not our imagination–at least not my imagination. I'm not making this stuff up."

He also presented a theory about his most recent supernatural sensations at Bedford Hall. Admittedly not a student of the paranormal, he was amazed when he learned how his thoughts paralleled those of long-time "ghost hunters."

He said there has seemed to be a heightened level of activity at Bedford since it was drastically renovated recently. "We had all kinds of strange things happen there, and we chalk them up to the ghost or ghosts.

"Maybe you think it's silly," he added, "but I personally believe the spooks got P.O'd because their old home was being changed. Things got really weird in the garage, or the carriage house, when they made that art studio there. I think it upset the ghost!"

No, sir, I don't think it's silly. In my 35+ years of investigating hauntings, many or most seemed to intensify during or after renovations or modifications to a structure. The simplest explanation is that the work has stirred up the spirits, or has opened (or closed) points of ingress or egress through which the energies may (or may not) pass.

That could account for the activity in Bedford Hall, and similar reports of ghostly goings-on at the Sturdevant Hall on South Franklin Street.

Itself a composite of what were two separate buildings, Sturdevant is said to be haunted by several ghosts, according to those who have lived or worked within its walls.

Disembodied footfalls have often been heard when the building was otherwise quite and empty. The distinct, pungent aroma of stale cigar smoke has wafted through at least one room there, and other signs that one is never really alone there have surfaced throughout the years.

Likewise at the conjoined Chesapeake and Delaware residence halls, and untold other buildings on Wilkes' historic–and haunted campus.

The West Mountain Sanitarium

It would be folly to publish a book about haunted places in Luzerne and Lackawanna counties and not mention the West Mountain Sanitarium.

After all, the ruins high in the hills in Ransom Township, Lackawanna County, have long been the darling of those who venture there in search of the many ghosts that are said to swirl in eternal agony. Or, so the stories go.

One Internet yarn has spun totally out of control: "During a massive fire," the blurb claims, "hundreds of patients died and are believed to haunt the place."

Really?

There have been fires–several of them–at the abandoned complex. They have largely been set by vandals and/or thrill seekers who ventured onto the condemned property.

But, the legends persist about the grounds being soaked with spirits that roam by day and night. And, perhaps they are.

The first sanitarium was built there in the early 20th century and replaced by a larger facility in 1932. It housed what were sometimes called "lungers," or patients stricken by the "white plague" of what was then called consumption or, as we know it, tuberculosis.

The latter sanitarium (and no, it was not an "asylum," as some tales have called it) housed a bit more than 100 patients, so if "hundreds died" in the alleged great fire there, well, do the math.

After its closing in 1974, the sanitarium tumbled into ruin as swiftly as the stories of its ghosts began to escalate. And, as the curious wandered onto the site looking for ghosts–or whatever–it became a vulnerable and endangered hangout. Firefighters were called often to quell blazes there set either intentionally or accidentally. By the turn of the 20th century, it had become a dilapidated wreck.

It is highly likely that ghostly energies indeed do permeate the grounds of the old institution. So much trauma and so much drama certainly did leave their imprints there. There is little doubt that it is, then, haunted.

One interesting note from the history of the West Mountain Sanitarium involves a Honesdale man named Dick Smith, and has nothing to do with ghosts.

Born in 1901, Smith contracted TB in 1931, just as his career as a songwriter was taking off. He was admitted to West Mountain where, during his treatment, he continued to write lyrics.

One particular song he penned was given to Felix Bernard, who wrote the music for it. It received some notice, but never became popular during Smith's lifetime. On September 28, 1935, Dick Smith died at the sanitarium high above West Scranton.

Eight years later, his song became a "hit," and since then, it has become a true standard. You probably know the words. But, you probably didn't know that Dick Smith, while a patient at West Mountain Sanitarium, wrote the words to "Winter Wonderland.

(Photos courtesy of www.abandonedbutnotforgotten.com)

CAR 46

When you board streetcar No.46 at the Electric City Trolley Museum in downtown Scranton, stop, look, and listen.

Are you alone?

Is that sighing, or perhaps snoring that you hear?

Can you feel the presence? Can you sense the spirit?

In streetcar No. 46, you are not alone. Someone, sometime, somewhere boarded that trolley and never left. New Orleans has its "Streetcar Named Desire." Scranton has its

Streetcar Named *Haunted.*

Some staff members and volunteers at the museum were a bit put off when they learned that a ghost remains planted in one of the seats of No. 46. Others welcomed the spirit, hoped she was comfortable, and wished her well on her eternal ride.

There have been numerous reports of ghostly activity in the building, mostly from young volunteers who spend time there. Events range from just "creepy feelings" to genuine, classic poltergeist activity including, but not limited to items moving on their own and the hushed sound of voices.

There are a dozen or so historic trolleys on display at the Electric City Trolley Museum, and many more in its storage and restoration facilities.

Situated on the edge of the Steamtown National Historic Site grounds, the museum is the work of a dedicated group of individuals committed to preserving the history of streetcars and trolleys. While much of the museum focuses directly onto lines that fanned out from Scranton, many of the cars on view are from transit companies and authorities throughout eastern Pennsylvania and, for the most part, Philadelphia and its suburban lines.

One of those cars is the Philadelphia & Western Railway car No. 46.

Built in 1907 by the St. Louis Car Co., it is the last of the first generation of cars that ran on a third-rail line from Philadelphia's 69th Street Station into Norristown and other suburbs.

It had been converted into a work car in 1928 and retired in 1976. It was meticulously restored and returned to its original elegance. It is among the very best in the collection at the museum.

In 2006, a casual visitor to the museum was heading out when he turned his attention to the volunteer at the souvenir desk and popped the question.

He asked if there have ever been reports of any "vibes" in the museum.

The volunteer requested a clearer definition of the word "vibes."

He then shocked the attendant by calmly revealing that he had detected the spirit of a woman in Car 46. "She's just sitting in there, by herself, waiting for a ride."

The volunteer giggled a bit, but the visitor would have none of that. He said he was quite serious, and that the old Philadelphia streetcar was haunted.

At least one other self-described "psychic" has also claimed that a lonesome female spirit occupies a seat in Car 46. She told this writer that the energy seems strongest near the rear of the car, and it may be the ghost of a woman who either died in the car or was stricken with a serious health problem while riding on it and passed away after being removed from it by medical personnel.

She's sad, lonely, and her spirit is likely to never leave the confines of the car, according to the psychic. "It's a textbook 'residual' energy," she noted. "She's sort of locked in there, with nowhere else to go."

The Ghostly Horses of Harvey's Lake

Myths and legends at Harvey's Lake run as deep as the water there. Murders...scandals...even shipwrecks have spiced the history of the 600-acre natural lake.

Add to those elements even more mysteries such as the giant creature said to lurk in the depths of the lake and the once-trusted belief that the lake was indeed bottomless.

And, oh yes, then there is the story of the ghostly horses of Harvey's Lake.

The lake's very namesake is the stuff of legend. It is said that Plymouth native Benjamin

Harvey was a prisoner of the British during the Revolutionary War. He was freed by the king's army in upstate New York, but was destined for an dismal fate at the hands of the local natives.

One story has it that the tribal chief set up an aboriginal firing squad of a sort when he tied Harvey to a tree, armed three of his best warriors with tomahawks, and ordered them to hurl them at the condemned man.

Miraculously, each tomahawk missed its mark. The chief believed it was a calling from above and spared Harvey's life.

It was on his way back to Plymouth when Harvey "discovered" the big lake that later took his name.

But what of that story of a monstrous critter that swims in the depths of Harvey's Lake? Not true, say those who have studied, fished, dived, or lived on the banks of the lake. Just a fable, they say.

Those folks also discount the old saw that the lake is bottomless. It is Pennsylvania's largest natural lake in water volume, but as the late Harvey's Lake SCUBA diver once said, "if it has no bottom, what holds the water up?"

"Indeed, there were rumors the lake had deep springs which were connected by mysterious channels to the Finger Lakes in central New York State," said historian, author, and attorney F.

Charles Petrillo. "However, the lake was sounded in the early years of the twentieth century and the deepest point was 90 to 100 feet."

One tale that won't go away as easily, however, is that of the ghost horses.

"The most persistent legend, which still continues," Petrillo said, "is that there is preserved in the cold depths of the lake bottom two horses which had fallen through the ice in the dim past.

"Interviews with the oldest residents of the lake, from the World War I era, confirm this legend and may have arisen as early as the late 1800s.

"The legend is generally that a team of horses used for ice-harvesting broke through the ice one winter and sank to the bottom. Their ghostly remains are still there and preserved by the frigid water. Most claim the event occurred near Alderson not far from the deepest section of the lake between the picnic ground and Point Breeze."

There is no documentation of any ice-cutting accident that may have resulted in the deaths of a team of horses on the lake.

But, as Petrillo added, "The undated accident which gave rise to the legend is likely a true event–although not likely to have been reported in area newspapers." He speculated that it probably happened in the 1890s.

And, he felt it was unlikely that the remains

of any animals that drowned in the lake would be preserved, despite the depth and temperature of the water.

Still, the lake does hold its secrets.

"There are also four drowning victims whose bodies have never been recovered from the lake bottom," he noted.

"In 1898 two young men, Gowan C. Herdman and Lewis McCarter were riding horses in the shallow water near Alderson when one of the horses stumbled and in the ensuing panic both boys were drowned. It is possible that at least the former story was embellished over the years to create the legend of the lost horses."

Serious efforts have been made by divers to locate any sunken ice sled and possible equine remains in the lake, but to no avail.

All the research, all the dives, and all the science will never–and, by all that is right, *should* never–erase from the history of Harvey's Lake the *mystery* of Harvey's Lake.

Should you be on the shores of the big lake under a full moon some night, see a pair of sturdy steeds rise from the water, and hear their whinnying echo in the night, you will know that at least one of those legends of that lake is quite–and frighteningly–true.

THE ETERNAL ICE CUTTERS

Our next story takes us to another body of water and another tale of ghostly ice cutters.

In this story, the setting is the Susquehanna River and the ghosts are human, not horses.

Jim Bach, a longtime businessman and resident of Shickshinny has lived through many of the floods and changes that have challenged the riverside town.

He is dearly interested in the past, present, and future of Shickshinny, and recalled for this

61

book what is Shickshinny's most enduring ghost story.

"They actually built a road at the end of Butler Street that went right into the river," he said, while showing me a vintage map/sketch of the roadway.

"They would drive their carriages onto that extension of Butler Street and load them with ice carved from the frozen Susquehanna."

As in Harvey's Lake, there is a story about an ill-fated ice-carving crew that met wet deaths. In Shickshinny, though, the victims were humans, not horses.

Not realizing that the ice was too thin to continue their work, two workers plunged through and under the ice. Their bodies were swept downstream and never found.

To this day, when conditions are right, their ghostly forms can be seen rising from the river at the end of Butler Street, just beyond a buffer of trees at Crary Park.

ANN'S APPARITION

There are those at the Nathan Denison House who don't want you to know this, but there are others who will readily concede that a ghost walks within the walls of the historic site in Forty Fort.

It is, most of those who have felt or seen her believe, the ghost of Ann Denison, daughter of Nathan and Elizabeth (Betsy) Denison.

The Denisons and their homestead are intricately intertwined with the Wyoming Valley. Nathan was one of the forty men who were sent to garrison a fort (hence the town's name, Forty Fort) in the valley and went on to play a major role in the Battle of Wyoming and as a judge and legislator in the newly-formed Commonwealth of Pennsylvania.

Thus, the pedigree of the Denison House as a certified Pennsylvania Historical and Museum Commission site was assured by Denison's upstanding service to his community.

Following the Revolution, Denison also became a civic and business leader and a family man. He and Betsy entertained regularly in their clapboard house fashioned after the Denison homestead in New England.

Today, that house is revered as the oldest (1790) house in town and the former home of one of its most respected settlers.

That the ghostly denizen of the Denison is Ann is pure speculation, but those who have pieced together the paranormal puzzle there believe it is she.

Informative and interesting tours are offered at the house from May to August, and it is on one of these interpretive treks where Ann's spirit may be felt, and even seen.

No one really know why Ann's ghost remains locked inside her family's old house.

There is some evidence that Ann may have been pregnant while living there and may have suffered a medical problem related to that pregnancy. Another unsubstantiated story, but one that has been passed down through several generations, is that the unfortunate and quite pregnant Ann suffered not a medical condition but a tumble down the stairs from the second floor.

Although she did not die as the result of the fall, the trauma of the accident was strong enough to leave an imprint of her energy within the walls of the Denison House.

Guides at the historic site have reported catching a fleeting glimpse of a young woman at the top of the stairs when they were certain no one was on the second floor. One volunteer said she was standing at the base of the staircase, alone, when she distinctly heard the creepy, creaky footfall of phantom feet on the floorboards of the stairs. One by one, slowly, the footsteps made their way to the second floor until the sound seemed to fade away.

The photograph at the beginning of this story is not a picture of the ghost, nor is it meant to represent it. It is, however, a picture of a mannequin on the second floor of the Denison House.

A visitor who had never been to the house told the story of being impressed with the authenticity of the costume on a young woman she had seen standing at the top of the staircase to the second floor. She assumed the woman in a creamy white, vintage dress was a tour guide or a reenactor.

The guide dismissed the comment and in an automatic reflex thanked the visitor for her comments. However, a walk to the second floor satisfied both the guide and the visitor that there was nobody else in the house at the time.

Then, the visitor who swears she saw the figure of a young woman standing at the top of the steps entered the room in which the mannequin in the accompanying photo is situated.

She recoiled and said that the dress on the mannequin looked familiar–*hauntingly* familiar. She said that unless that mannequin is capable of walking, she's sure she saw a ghost in the Denison House that day.

THE BEETLE IN THE NIGHT

In my long career of gathering, writing, and telling ghost stories, none quite like this one has ever come along. But, as with so many other stories submitted to me, I have no reason to discredit them. My philosophy is to allow the reader to conclude what they may.

The setting for this story is the rambling hillside grounds of Penn State Hazleton Campus. Propped on the western ridge of Buck Mountain overlooking the Drums Valley, the core of the campus is the 26-acre property that was purchased by PSU in 1948.

It was the estate of Eckley Markle, a local coal baron who called his home, appropriately, "Highacres."

Markle's mansion became the "old main" of PSU-Hazleton, and is presently the administration building of the lovely campus.

Many changes have been made on the campus since 1976, but the general lay of the land around the old Markle Mansion remains the same.

It was in 1976 that the story submitted by Penn State alum Ron Drum took place. It has lingered with him for all these years, and his recollections were submitted in such a fine narrative that they may stand as he sent them.

It would be nice if any ghost story from the Hazleton campus of Penn State was set in the old Markle mansion, as it is one of those buildings that *looks* as if it should be haunted. But alas, the spook–or whatever it was–of this story is not your garden-variety "ghost in the mansion on the high, windy hill" type. It is a...well...keep reading.

"I have to admit," Mr. Drum wrote, "I have told it a few times to young people gathered around an evening campfire." It is indeed the kind of story that would have young minds watching and listening as they settled in for a dark night in a campground.

The Hazleton native also confessed that although the details of the story sound a tad far-fetched, every one of those details is reported as they played out one very weird night on the campus.

The cast of characters includes two students and the campus police chief. Their names have been changed at Mr. Drum's request. Brad and Jim, as we shall call them, were members of the "student patrol" club on campus and were called on to help out with security at campus functions and to patrol the grounds.

"Both of the students were very well known within the PSU-Hazleton community," he continued, "and might not be very happy to learn this story had become public knowledge. They kept the story fairly quiet. It was just too crazy!"

Crazy? You be the judge.

"On the night of this story," he began, "Todd arrived on campus sometime after midnight. He was a security guard at a factory in the Valmont Industrial Park, a short distance from the campus. When his shift at the plant ended, he would walk to the campus.

"The police officer on duty usually let him into the Commons where he would sleep until classes started in the morning. If he was unable to find the police officer on duty and the night was warm and dry, he would climb the tree beside the Commons and nap in a natural hammock created by two of the tree's branches.

That night, Todd could not immediately locate the officer and fell asleep in the hammock.

"He was not sure how long he slept, but he was awakened by the sound of a car parking beneath him. He looked down and realized it was

Jim in the campus patrol car so he climbed down and got in. Jim was usually happy to see Todd but on this evening he was a bit preoccupied."

Jim was also a bit unsettled. I defer to Ron Drum's account of the conversation Todd and Jim might have had:

"What's the matter?" Todd asked.

"Probably nothing," Jim replied, "but something just happened that I can't figure out," Jim responded.

"What's that?" Todd continued.

"Well, you know how I always check the campus out when I start my shift?"

"Yup, you drive the whole campus from back to front."

"That's right, I don't want any surprises."

"I know what you mean! Any problems tonight?"

"Just one. I got surprised."

"How so?"

"I made my rounds like I always do, then I came back up here and parked. That's when I heard it."

"Heard what?"

"The sound of a car, coming from the back of the campus, where a car should not have been. Suddenly, I saw this powder blue Volkswagen coming at me and he was moving! He was past me before I could get the car started. He turned the

curve at the lookout as I pulled out of here. He was gone by the time I turned the second curve. I don't know where he went. I even checked down in the trees to see if he ran off the road! Since I didn't find anything, I came back here."

At about that point in their conversation, Jim held up his hand for quiet.

"Listen," Jim said, *"there it is again, coming this way!"*

"I hear it," Todd responded.

As Jim was starting the patrol car, the VW sped past them. Jim and Todd were in pursuit. Around one, and then a second curve, they followed the VW, but all along the way the "Beetle" was out of their sight. They looked in parking lots, behind buildings, and everywhere a car–even a small car–could be secreted.

All along, each young man knew that what they had seen and heard was well beyond the bounds of reality. Both were certain there were no other cars driving on that campus that night. And, the more they thought about it, the more that VW seemed a bit out of the ordinary.

The idea of this being a ghost had by now crossed both of their minds. Both had dismissed the thought as ridiculous. Neither told the other of this strange idea.

Each holding within themselves their gut feelings about what they might be experiencing,

Todd and Jim had no idea that the best (or worst) was yet to come.

Everything grew very quiet and still. Then it all began again. Off in the distance, from the back of the campus where a car should not be–COULD NOT BE–came the sound that was now familiar to both–vroom, vroom!

Jim started the cruiser's engine.

"Todd, hang on because I'm going to ram the son-of-a-bitch!"

True to his word, Jim slammed his foot on the gas just as the car reached them.

Both swear there was no way Jim could have missed the VW, but he did.

Both said it was if the VW had passed right through them!

Todd searched the bumper for a license plate but could not find one. He tried to see if it was a man or woman driving, but the rear window was black, as if painted over.

Jim did his best to keep on the VW's tail, almost losing control on the first curve. Todd kept his eyes on the VW. The car was NOT getting away again!

Todd saw the VW go around the second curve. Jim was right on his tail, again almost losing control again around the second curve. Then, he slammed on the brakes, screeching to a halt, sliding halfway down the hill.

The road ahead was clear, all the way down to the entrance of the campus. Nothing!

Both Jim and Todd yelled at the same time, "WHERE DID IT GO?"

The befuddled student patrolmen looked everywhere. There was no sight of the Volkswagen, and no rational explanation for its apparent disappearance.

If, that is, it ever existed in the first place!

Mr. Drum continued:

The sky was now growing lighter as the morning was fast approaching.

"I guess we better head back to the office. I've got reports to file," Jim suggested.

"Are you going to include the VW?" asked Todd.

"No, no way, Todd. I'm not telling ANYONE about this, and neither are you!"

"OK, not a word, but I AM going to figure this out someday," Todd promised.

The mood was congenial in the campus police office that morning as Ron Drum and another student reported to work. But, Jim and Todd were in no mood for congeniality. They both probably chafed at the bit to tell the story of the phantom Volkswagen.

Ron Drum did acknowledge that both of the young men liked a good laugh, but didn't think of them as practical jokesters. "I do not believe that either would have made up a story such as this."

In fact, Todd and Jim didn't keep their secret too long at all.

There is one more piece of the story to tell.

As the four of us were just sitting down with our cups of coffee, the office door slammed open. The campus police chief was booming as he entered: "Hey, Jim! I thought you said the campus was clear!" (meaning that no one was on the campus).

"I did," Jim fired back. "It is," he nervously said as he glanced at Todd. Todd looked away.

"Then explain how come I was almost just run over by some knucklehead in a Volkswagen," the chief barked. "It came speeding up on me from the back of the campus. In fact, I'm not sure how he missed me. He was gone before I could get into the cruiser, but he better not come back. I'll ring his neck!"

With that, Todd and Jim looked at each other and related the details of the previous night's chase after what they were now convinced was a ghost car.

To my knowledge, neither Todd nor Joe ever figured out what happened that night. I am also not aware of anyone else ever reporting having seen the VW again. If they have seen it, they didn't tell anyone. Would you?"

The Coach Room at the Historic Stage Coach Inn

ETERNAL GUESTS AT THE STAGE COACH INN?

Do the bottles behind the bar contain the only spirits at the Historic Stage Coach Inn on Route 309 between Drums and Mountain Top?

That depends on whom you ask.

Some will flatly and nervously deny that they work among spirits of the ghostly kind. Others will readily admit that they have sensed or even seen the ghostly guests who are spending an eternity in the lovely and truly historic hillside inn.

To appreciate the history of the place, one

75

must peel back its 21st, 20th, and even a good portion of the 19th century trappings and imagine the time so long ago when a crude old Indian pathway called the Nanticoke Trail climbed Butler Mountain.

It would take the old Beaver Meadows Stage Coach some five tortuous hours to make the trip from Beaver Meadows, through Hazleton, and to Wilkes-Barre. Along the way was "Sand Springs," a welcome oasis where passengers and horses would find fresh spring water.

That water pause evolved into an overnight stop and eventually, in 1946 after what is now Route 309 was built, a restaurant whose name honored the old stage coach stop.

The Historic Stage Coach Inn was purchased by Ed and Betty Deets in 1988, and they made many improvements in what had already become a Luzerne County landmark.

To get an "official" take on the alleged haunting of the inn, we went to Ed Deets' office in Mountain Top, from which he governs his business empire.

That office is adorned with the trappings of the social, civic, and political lives Deets has led throughout his illustrious life.

But, Mr. Deets–what of the Historic Stage Coach Inn? Are there ghosts there?

His response could be summed up in one

word–"yes."

I have always maintained that the presence of a ghost or two adds character to a place. And, although the character of the Stage Coach Inn needs no ghosts to enhance it, there are entities that glide through its dining rooms.

Ed Deets has heard the stories, and is not hesitant to offer that he believes at least one of the eternal guests there is a former owner who passed over in what was then his living quarters and is now the "Coach Room" of the sprawling restaurant.

Ed recalled that the immediate past owner, too, had reported spirit activity in the restaurant. That could indicate the presence of more than one ghost in the building.

It is all but certain that there have been two, and perhaps three deaths of natural causes inside the building. A carriage accident many years ago is also believed to have claimed a life in what is now the upper parking lot.

The imprints of their energies are what remain there today, and forever. And, a sensitive mortal who settles in for a fine dinner may just be joined by one of the benign, but occasionally restless wraiths that ramble from time to time in that historic–and, yes–*haunted* Stage Coach Inn.

The "Patriotic Room" at the Muddy Moose

Emily, The Ethereal Entity of the Muddy Moose

In the 35 years I have been investigating, collecting, and reporting ghost stories, I have often had to work hard to convince people to allow their stories to be published. I understand the hesitance of people to publicly reveal that their homes or businesses are haunted.

But never, ever, anywhere, did I have to get the approval of a *building* before I published its story.

Well, that's not exactly how it happened. I actually and unknowingly had an intermediary get the approval.

I had spoken with Karen Podrasky about what I had heard was a good ghost story in her delightful Muddy Moose Country Store on Main Street in Laflin.

Karen cautiously outlined the story for me in a telephone call. But, she urged me to visit her store to truly understand and perhaps experience what many others have experienced there.

I was greeted at the door by the ebullient, effervescent woman who rescued a century-plus old miners' boarding house and assembled a wonderland of decorative, gift, and collectible items.

Karen has become so much at one with the splendid old building that she speaks to it.

And, the splendid old building speaks back!

"I did that about you," she said. "I was standing at the front door with my husband and I asked the building if it was OK for me to let you use the story about our ghosts in a book.

"As soon as I asked, a jar of shredded wax used in candlemaking fell off a shelf next to me."

By doing that, the jar seemed to defy all conventional knowledge of gravity. And, Karen took it as an affirmative response from the building—or from Emily, or Frank, or Raymond. It was fine with them to reveal the secrets of the store to the inquiring author.

Those three are among the entities that inhabit the Muddy Moose and have free reign of the 15 themed rooms of merchandise—and the one room that remains locked at all time.

We shall visit that locked room later. First, let us go back to 2003 when Karen and husband Len embarked on their adventure.

"When we first bought the house," she said, "there were noises and many different things happening." The couple wrote it all off as the quirks of construction and the rumblings of renovation.

But early on, Karen felt she was never really alone there. There were the standard sensations of chilly winds on warm days, warm spots on cold days, etc. But, more significant and provocative events began to unfold, and Karen came to believe that there was at least one playful ghost in her midst.

Local "ghost hunters" and a trusted medium confirmed that there were energies there, and

Karen merely shrugged knowingly.

"How do I explain it," she questioned. "Customers have watched wreaths literally fly through the air from the wall to the floor. Those things *just don't do that,* if you know what I mean."

A local doctor was in the shop chatting with Karen in the main room when a bar of soap lofted from the shelf and struck the man on the shoulder on its way to the floor.

"He told me, 'You know, Karen, I'm a man of science. What just happened was physically impossible!'"

Karen agreed, scolded Emily, and went on with the conversation. The good doctor continued to look over his shoulder nervously, as if awaiting Emily's next move.

Emily is the friskiest of the entities in the building. Karen believes she is Emily Morgan, who died of consumption at the age of nine in that very building.

Karen has established a strong psychic connection with Emily. Early in that relationship, Karen believed the little girl had blonde, curly hair and wore a white dress in her eternal ramblings through her store. When someone donated a vintage picture of a group of children to her, her eyes went directly to one of the little girls. "That is Emily," she exclaimed. Her medium friend confirmed her conclusion. "I don't know how I knew," she sighed.

The Pittston native has heard many casual visitors and customers remark about the comfortable feeling inside the building. "And," she said, "people who are in tune with all of this come in here regularly and tell me there is 'something in this house' or that they 'feel something' here. I just smile and nod."

Emily's housemates aren't as active as she. The entity identified as "Raymond" was likely a boarder there in the late 1800s. His presence has been described as that of a rugged individualist with a kind heart.

"Frank" is believed to have been a handyman in the boarding house, perhaps as late as the 1920s. While Emily is an innocent, gentle spirit, Frank may be a bit more assertive.

Of the three, Frank may be the one who has fidgeted with things in the house and stirred up commotion on physical and psychic levels.

One incident in her beloved store stands out above all others as a baffling mystery.

"We were painting woodwork upstairs," she remembered. "I was up there and the painter was on the first floor. I stood at the top of the stairs and told the painter that I'd love to crackle the paint in the Patriotic Room.

"I came downstairs for a break, and then

went back upstairs. All of the woodwork and doors were crackled!"

The natural explanation would have been that the painter went upstairs and did the crackling.

But, he did not.

Perhaps, then, paint that had been previously applied just shriveled, wrinkled, and crackled itself.

It did not.

"We couldn't think of any explanation," Karen continued. "Crackling just doesn't happen. There is a technique to it. And, that woodwork was crackled."

Karen was astonished. The painter apparently felt another emotion.

"We didn't see him again after that," she laughed. "He left his paints and his supplies here and hightailed it out of here."

So, what about that "locked room" at the top of the stairs–a room used only for storage and off-limits to the public?

"That was Emily's room," Karen said. Although usually filled from wall-to-wall, ceiling-to-floor with stored items, the room occasionally echoes with Emily's ethereal activities.

She was in the room below Emily's room one quiet evening just after closing time, talking with a customer. The solitude was broken by a repetitive thumping sound coming from the second floor. "That was just Emily up there," Karen said, "bouncing a ball. I told her to 'knock it off,' and the bouncing sound stopped."

She and others who have probed the paranormal atmosphere in the Muddy Moose believe that the locked room may hold the vortex from which the swirl of supernatural activity emanates. Generally, that activity is benign. But, there have been occasions when the ghosts were grumpy, so to speak.

Karen was in that room and was about to lift up a floor board to get to some pipes when she experienced a furious flurry of activity. "You would have thought that we released a demon from hell," she laughed. She placed the floor board back in place and left the room, apologizing to Emily for the intrusion.

Karen is both sensitive and sensible. At first a confirmed nonbeliever in ghosts, Emily and the others have changed her mind. She has grown comfortable with her elusive guests. After all, she reasons, they were there a long time before she was.

"It does give me chills every once in a while," she admitted. "But," she laughed, "I just tell them to get away from me, and they do."

"It's all part of me now."

☗

A Haunting Whodunit at the Houdini Museum

Harry Houdini remains as fascinating today as he was during his brilliant career as a magician, illusionist, and escape artist. Not many places on earth pay more tribute to Houdini than the Houdini Museum at 1433 N. Main Street in Scranton.

Few performers in history have been as enigmatic as Houdini. His birth name was Erik (or Ehrich) Weiss (or Weisz). He was born March 24 (or April 6), 1874 in Budapest, Hungary (or Appleton, Wisconsin).

He was a self-proclaimed psychic investigator who did not believe in psychic investigation. He did not think it was possible to communicate with the dead, but ordered that a seance be staged at his grave on the anniversary of his death, Halloween, 1926.

Did he believe in ghosts? Would he tell you if he did?

While this story involves a ghost at the Houdini Museum, Houdini is but a bit player. It is more a story of 1433 N. Main St. and its resident ghost, Walter Roberson.

At least that's who Dick Brooks believes haunts the building that houses his museum and theater.

Brooks and his partner, Dorothy Dietrich, operated the Magic Towne House on the upper east side of Manhattan for 15 years. But, as real estate costs in that neighborhood and throughout New York City skyrocketed, they fled the Big Apple for the Electric City in the mid-1980s. Both seasoned magicians and performers, Dick and Dorothy combined those skills with Brooks' vast collection of Houdiniana and set up the museum and

"Psychic Theater."

Little did they realize that the psychic element would be more than "theater."

The Houdini Museum, 1433 N. Main St., Scranton

"When we bought the building it was dilapidated," Brooks said. "Everybody in the neighborhood knew it was haunted, so nobody wanted to buy it. The real estate agent handed us the key and said, 'I don't know why you're interested in this building. I won't even set foot in it!'"

Brooks was actually interested in the building because it *looked* haunted. And, it wasn't long until he came to realize that it *was* haunted.

The building had served many masters over the years. Brooks learned that it had been a grocery store, ice cream parlor, and disco, among other things. After settling in, Brooks gutted the inside and proceeded to rebuild it using as much original material as possible. He showed me a framed photograph of the building as it appeared before he restored it. "Every time I hung this on the wall, it fell off and the glass shattered. I gave up. Maybe it has something to do with the ghosts here."

The Bethlehem, Pa. native was in tune with the paranormal world early in life and was prepared for whatever the building and its occupants would throw at him.

"I used to do psychic stuff when I was a kid," Brooks said in a New York accent that had swept away any hints of his Pennsylvania youth. He added that he, like Houdini, was also fascinated with the late 19th/early 20th century phenomenon of Spiritualism. His personal questions about all of it emerged as professional answers in his psychic shows and seances. But, it took some adjustment when he realized that his new venue held many secrets.

"Some strange things started to happen and I got kind of spooked," he said. "When we took this place over, we would work until midnight or so and we'd hear sounds here. Those sounds led us to the attic, where we found a lot of information about incidents that happened in this building."

Brooks claimed that most of those incidents revolved around one man, whose entity remains firmly entrenched in the building

"I would have dreams about the guy," he said. "It was like he was trying to take me over."

That "guy," said Brooks, is Walter Roberson. According to documents Brooks said he discovered in the attic, Roberson was a teacher and professor whose career was cut short when his wife found out about his numerous dalliances with students and, in a drunken rage, jammed a hat pin in his eyes, blinding him. Astonishingly, Roberson refused to press charges against his wife.

Instead, the couple lived uneasy lives in their house. Brooks' findings indicate that when Roberson's eyesight was savagely taken from him, another sense–a sixth sense–kicked in. He managed to carve out a living as a psychic reader and counselor.

Some neighbors were wary of Roberson's newfound "talents" and even his wife discredited them as "fake voodoo."

Still, people from a wide area came to

Roberson for consultation.

Walter would be a prime candidate as the residual energy in the Houdini Museum if only for his spiritual connections. But, there is more to the story...much more.

Walter Roberson. Photo provided by and courtesy of Dick Brooks and the Houdini Museum.

Undated and undocumented information provided by Dick Brooks to this author indicated that both Roberson and his wife were found dead at the North Main Street building, victims of an apparent murder-suicide. Martha Roberson's body was discovered in the attic of the building, her throat slashed with a steak knife. Walter's body was found inside a car at the rear of the building. Both had been dead for several days.

When news of the horrible crime broke, more stories surfaced about the building's lurid past.

Local legend had it that the building was built on the site of an Indian burial ground, and was thus cursed. And, it was also revealed that two workers died during construction of the building.

He told of a recent seance there during which a 20-something woman shook, cried, and screamed during the seance show he presents. She was not necessarily impacted by the show, but by the ghosts in the building. Her boyfriend actually won a wrist watch as a prize during the show. "His girlfriend demanded that he not take it," Brooks said. "She told him she didn't want anything from this building, and hustled him out."

"Oh," Brooks said with conviction, "there's something going on here, and that's for sure!"

Fact? Fantasy? Do not forget for one minute that at his Houdini Museum, Dick Brooks spins intricate illusions. But, he maintains, the ghosts of that museum are quite real.

☗

THE POLTERGEIST IN THE PUB

Andy Gavin's Eatery and Pub is one of those "Cheers" kind of places where Scrantonians have gathered for decades.

For nearly two of those decades, Don Surace has owned the Green Ridge landmark, and the pleasant publican will readily admit that even after his 1392 N. Washington Avenue hotspot closes its doors, one permanent patron lingers in the darkness.

Yes, there are living, breathing beings in the building. They occupy an apartment on the third floor. But no, they are not the subjects of this story.

That would be Andy Gavin's resident ghost.

"I hadn't really known much about the ghost until I actually bought the place," Don said. "My former partner and I were at a party and some people looked at me and said I'd never rent the apartment upstairs. I asked them why, and they told me it was haunted. I said, 'Get outta here!' They said they were one-hundred percent serious. They proceeded to tell us stories about things that had happened to them there."

Undaunted by that revelation about his new

acquisition, Don dug in to build his business. He even rented that upstairs apartment with little problem.

However, the words of warning from that individual early on continued to haunt him. Soon, the ghost itself haunted him.

"During the years I've owned the building," he continued, "I've seen and experienced lots of things. It's always like someone's here, watching over me. Maybe it's just in my head, but when I'm in my office downstairs, I often feel as if someone is just over my shoulder, or walking past the door."

There have been more profound incidents there, too.

One night after the bar closed, a newspaper reporter was hanging around, and as Don was sweeping up, the reporter asked if the ghost stories about the place were true. He seemed a bit on edge.

"I asked him why he asked about the ghosts," Don said. "He told me he believed the ghost just touched him. And, to see an expression on somebody's face and to seem him turn pasty white like he did...oh, yeah, I was convinced he was serious!" The reporter claimed that someone had touched him on the shoulder three times, and nobody was anywhere nearby.

The folks at Andy Gavin's have given their

ghost the arbitrary name of "George." Beyond the classic unexplainable events that take place there, just about anything that goes wrong is blamed on George. But, some occurrences there go beyond the norm and into the paranormal zone.

Don was standing next to a dishwashing machine one night when he casually asked George for a sign. All of a sudden, the sprayer washer moved. Startled, Don asked George if he's really there, to do that again. George did that again.

He has heard mysterious music coming from no apparent source, seen objects move on their own, and has put up with numerous reports from employees and patrons when George is on the prowl.

"I had a cook quit on me one night because things kept falling over in the kitchen. He blamed it on the ghost and wanted no part of it."

There have been reports of strange episodes in the men's room when someone washing their hands would hear a toilet flush and notice a toilet stall open, as if someone was exiting the stall. Nobody, needless to say, was existing the stall. Unless, that is, it was George.

A psychic friend of Don's confirmed that Andy Gavin's is haunted, but no baseline for the haunting has been determined. Don had heard rumors that there was a suicide on the third floor sometime since the building was erected in about

1903, but that has never been confirmed. He mused that the energies might be filtering in from the trauma and drama that took place over the years in the county jail, which is across the street.

Local paranormal investigators have conducted sessions there, and hope to continue to probe the building's innards for more conclusive evidence that it is haunted.

Don said he would define George more as a "poltergeist," and more of a nuisance than something to be feared.

"You tell some people that the place is haunted," he offered, "and they shrug and say 'Yeah, OK, whatever.' But, you know what? Until you experience it yourself you really can't know what it's like."

George may be benign spirit, but he may have a frisky side. "We had a new girl behind the bar," Don noted. "I was ten, maybe 15 feet away from her when she looked over at me all of a sudden and asked, 'How'd you do that?' I asked her how I did *what*? She said that someone just pinched her in the butt...three times! I said well, guess what–you just met George the ghost!"

THE SPIRIT
OF THE SISTER

"I love ghost stories."

That was the simple assertion of Barbara A. Hoffman, assistant professor of English at Marywood University in Scranton.

Thus, Prof. Hoffman isn't at all concerned that she teaches at what some believe is a haunted campus.

Of course, the presumed resident spirit at Marywood wouldn't hurt a fly. Scare it, perhaps, but not hurt it.

Heavy into local legends and lore, Prof. Hoffman once invited folklorist Brent Augustus to speak in what could be the epicenter of the energies from the beyond–Regina Hall.

Augustus, who is also a self-proclaimed parapsychologist and ghost hunter, was regaling his audience when to everyone's surprise and shock, the ghost may have entered the hall.

"While he was talking," Prof. Hoffman said, "a big, heavy, oak door opened and slammed shut. Then, an old grandfather's clock went off!"

What made those otherwise banal occurrences remarkable is that no (visible) body came through the door–and, that grandfather's clock had never made a sound as long as anyone could remember.

Until, that is, the ghost hunter invited by the woman who "loves ghost stories" set up shop in the residence hall/chapel building.

Prof. Hoffman, who has taught for nearly 40 years, has a very enlightened approach and attitude about whatever lies beyond. She has no problems reconciling her interest in the supernatural with her faith, and has been quoted as saying that after she passes on, she would be content to return to Marywood and haunt the campus, as a "good ghost."

Perhaps then, she will meet the spirit that many students say wanders the campus. It is that of a silent, gliding, kindly nun who has been in several buildings and locations throughout the campus.

Photographs with mysterious "orbs" have been taken by students, and they add a higher-tech fuel to the feeling that perhaps there really is a nun who so dearly loved Marywood's storied campus that she stayed on to haunt it...as a "good ghost."

Jitters in Jefferson Township

What was once an elementary school in Mount Cobb is now the Jefferson Township municipal building.

But, there are those who believe that at a lasting reminder of the building's previous life dwells in the corridors and chambers of the old building.

For years, several township employees and administrators have felt the presence of a deceased school janitor named Bill.

He is a kindly spirit, but the nature of his unfinished and eternal tasks in the building are such that he has stirred up enough of a ruckus from time to time to send some township workers scurrying from their desks. At least one of them declared that they were so uncomfortable in the building that they would rather work from home

Much of the untoward activity has been centered in the furnace room, but certain sensations and feelings have swirled around in other parts of the building.

They say that the furnace room was Bill's self-proclaimed "office" when he worked there. He was known to take pride in his job and in the building. One of his fundamental roles was to shovel coal into the furnace early in the morning to make it cozy warm for the students and teachers. And, of course, he would also have to carry the ashes out and dispose of them.

So, that old furnace room door got quite a workout back then. And, to this day, that door still opens and closes with no noticeably human aid–usually on particularly cold winter mornings.

Ironically, Bill died the same year the school was closed. For several years, the building was boarded up, reemerging eventually as the township hall.

That old wooden furnace room door was replaced by a sturdy steel door, and the coal furnace was switched to natural gas.

Perhaps those alterations sparked Bill's restlessness and his determination to protect his beloved building and make things interesting for those who spend any amount of time there.

It is a classic story of what may be quite natural incidents being blamed on the supernatural. Indeed, the opening of the door, the random noises, and the ever-present feeling that some invisible being is just over one's shoulder have led many to shrug off the idea that the Jefferson Township hall is haunted.

But, just as many others believe that Bill is still stoking the flames of the furnace, and the fires of their imaginations.

HIS SPIRIT LIVES ON

He was a Civil War veteran, a natural history scholar, a taxidermist, a businessman, a physician, among other things. But, Dr. Isaiah Fawkes Everhart's name lives on in Scranton as the benefactor of the Everhart Museum of Natural History, Science, and Art in Nay Aug Park.

Some believe not only Dr. Everhart's name lives on, but his spirit remains within the walls of the fine institution.

The good doctor stipulated in his 1905 will that a portion of his estate be used to establish and endow a museum. Two years later, while obviously still very much alive, he announced that the money would be freed up so the museum could be built during his lifetime. In 1908, the Everhart Museum was opened.

The galleries continued to fill up in the next three years, and plans were made to dedicate a handsome bronze statue of Dr. Everhart that had been placed near the entrance of the building.

The designated date for the dedication was May 25, 1911. Dr. Everhart died on May 25, 1911. But, he lived to see the dedication of the statue!

It seems that Dr. Everhart came to visit the museum a few days before the scheduled dedication. He fell down on a staircase and suffered a broken hip. The dedication ceremonies were moved to May 20th. Five days later, Dr. Everhart passed away.

Over the years, the filmy figure of a distinguished man has been reported as appearing mysteriously and disappearing just as mysteriously in the galleries and near the front entrance of the museum.

Cara A. Sutherland, executive director of the Everhart Museum, said she has heard bits and pieces of the stories, but could not elaborate.

A young man who asked to be identified only as "Josh" said he was walking the grounds of the museum in 2005 when there emerged before him a well-dressed gentleman who paid him no mind as he strolled silently toward the building.

"I know what you'll think when I tell you this," Josh said, "but I would swear on two stacks of bibles that this, this ghostly man just continued walking *toward* the museum and disappeared *into* the museum–right through the wall! That's the last I saw of him, but I know I'm not crazy, and I know what I saw."

Of course, Josh was not expecting to see a ghost while he was casually strolling on the Mulberry Street side of the building. "I'm not really into spooky stuff," he added. "At least, I wasn't then. But I had never experienced anything like that before. He just sort of materialized, which attracted my attention. Then, he walked toward the building and, I swear, *through* it!"

Josh, who had heard that we were seeking ghost stories from the area, also said he had never told his story to anyone before.

"I kept it to myself," he said. "Maybe it was just my imagination or a freak of the lighting or something–but I know deep inside me that it wasn't."

Perhaps even more significantly, Josh also said he had never heard that others had reported the spirit of Dr. Everhart in and around the museum.

While Dr. Everhart's gentle spirit continues to guard his legacy, it is said that tormented entities roam Nay Aug Park. Several ghosts of individuals who plunged to their deaths from bridges in the Nay Aug Gorge, not far from the museum are said to stroll the grounds of the park.

AVONDALE APPARITIONS?

The Avondale Mine Disaster of September 6, 1869 remains as one of the most horrific industrial disasters in American history and is still the worst anthracite mining tragedy in Pennsylvania history.

Fire, explosions, cave-ins, and toxic gases ravaged the colliery and then the shafts, and 108 miners perished. Two rescuers also died. Tales of the terrible affair stunned the world and–*don't we hear this after every mine disaster?*–led to legislation that would improve working and safety conditions in the coal mines of Pennsylvania and beyond.

Nineteenth-century coal miners were a superstitious lot, and long after the bodies were removed from the mine and work was resumed, some miners flatly refused to reenter the mine, ever, fearing the ghosts of their fallen brethren still haunted the tunnels.

Other miners actually demanded that the mine owners *remove the ghosts* before they would go back to work.

As mine owners were wont to do, they placated the surviving miners by "investigating" and "concluding" that the ghosts some miners truly believe they saw were actually the flares and flashes of miners lighting matches on their wet coats. The gurgling, moaning sounds the miners attributed to spirits were just water pumps and the wind.

But, the rumors persisted then...and now...that the Avondale Colliery site in Plymouth is still haunted by the restless souls of miners who died there.

Paranormal researchers who have probed the site have detected high levels of activity, captured "orbs" in countless photographs, and recorded "electronic voice phenomena" (EVP), which has convinced them that the earlier miners' suspicions were more than superstitions.

♥

Emily's B&B, Lattimer

Emily's Ghost

Emily's Bed & Breakfast is positioned prominently in the historic town of Lattimer. The B&B is itself an historic structure, built for Augustus W. Drake, the general superintendent of the A. Pardee coal Company colliery.

Lattimer was a small coal mining patch in 1897, the year its name was vaulted into the world news and history books.

On steamy September 10th, in the midst of a bitter miners' strike that spread across Coal Country, miners congregated at the Lattimer Mines in a show of solidarity. The Luzerne County sheriff and hundreds of "deputies" were also heading to Lattimer to challenge the strikers. Among those in the ranks of the deputies were dozens of men who were employed by area coal companies. And, among them was Augustus W. Drake.

Miners marching at Lattimer, 1897

What happened on that Friday afternoon has gone into the history books as the "Lattimer Massacre."

With no warning, and showing no mercy, the deputies blasted oncoming miners with volley after volley of rifle fire, described by the the *Philadelphia Inquirer* as "A human slaughter in which men were mowed down like grain stalks before a scythe, by the deadly bullets which stormed for fully two minutes."

When the carnage ended, 19 men were dead and 38 more were wounded.

It is an understatement that the text of a marker placed at the site of the slaughter assailed the action of the authorities and defended the miners:

"It was not a battle because they were not aggressive, nor were they defensive because they had no weapons of any kind and were simply shot down like so many worthless objects, each of the licensed life-takers trying to outdo the others in butchery."

Angela Fierro does not believe the spirit activity in her tranquil inn has anything to do with the unrest in Lattimer so many years ago, but she is intrigued by the possibility that she shares the stately home with an ever-present entity.

"It is a very peaceful inn," she said, "and whomever 'remains' here does not cause any strife. I don't know of any stories that may contribute to any causes for it to be lurking behind."

Born and raised in Lattimer, Angela purchased the home in 1996 and her dream of opening a B&B came true two years later, after considerable renovations.

__The monument to victims of the Lattimer Massacre.__

it was during those renovations when something inexplicable occurred and steered Angela's imagination toward the supernatural.

The 140-year old building was one of the first built in Lattimer. Between Augustus Drake's and her ownership, only three others have owned it. She bought it from folks who had owned it since the 1930s. Although the notion of ghosts never came up in the sale negotiations, the previous owners did admit that there were certain rooms in the house in which they felt uncomfortable.

She lived offsite while the building was being renovated. A neighbor called her one day to alert her that smoke alarms were going off in her house.

She hastened to the building to find out what was the matter, and discovered that steam surging through opened valves had caused the alarms to go off.

She had just papered every wall upstairs. Had the alarms not gone off, all of that wallpaper would have been permanently damaged.

The next day, her contractor looked at her askance as she told the story of the sounding of the alarms and the salvation of the wallpaper.

"He stared at me and said 'That's not possible.' He told me the alarms were up there, but they were not wired in. And, there were no batteries in the alarms.

"He said there was no way those alarms could have gone off. But, they did!"

Then, one of her very first guests had something interesting to tell her. "She said that she hoped I wouldn't think she was crazy, but her family has always had been sensitive, and they all agreed that there were many spirits in the house and they were happy to be there."

Angela never, as she said, "plants the seed" in a guest's mind that her inn may harbor a spirit. "And," she added, "it's not as if everyone who stays here says they experience something."

However, several visitors have volunteered

that they have detected an energy. "I find it somewhat uncanny that anyone who claims they have seen something describes it the same way," she said. "It is always a woman with either a long dress or nightgown."

And, although she has never had any profound experiences or sightings, she maintains a sense of adventure and awe. "I actually do feel that there is a presence in this home," she said.

The closest she came to actually having an experience there was a time she came home and smelled the distinctive odor of cigarette smoke. "I don't let anyone smoke in this home," she asserted. But, both she and then a group of friends confirmed that there was the odor of cigarette smoke in one of the rooms.

"I actually talked to them. I said, 'Please, quit smoking!' And, I've never smelled that smoke since."

She has been told that the female spirit there is gentle and content. That, of course, is music to the ears of Angela Fierro, who in addition to operating the B&B there, lives there.

"I feel that she takes care of the house," she said. "She really does like it here, just like that woman said."

And, she is so docile that she allowed Angela Fierro to be perhaps the first living being to convince a ghost to stop smoking!

111

Although graveyards are usually not haunted, it has long been held that at least two male spirits amble through the historic Hollenback Cemetery in Wilkes-Barre. One is said to be a tad cantankerous, the other a bit confused.

THE PHANTOM OF THE CINEMA

It started as the Hersker Theater when opened in 1915. It became the Key Theater in 1941. Then, it was the Hersker again; and then the Key again. At the time of the publication of this book, it is the Cinema & Drafthouse.

Whatever its name, the classic movie house

113

on W. Broad Street in Hazleton is likely to have at least one steady customer–the ghost that has been reported there by several employees over several years.

The current owner has heard some of the stories, but she declined to comment about them.

Previous operators, however, have reported seeing a motionless, shadowy figure standing to the right of the stage; another vague presence in the seating area; and still another lurking in the projection booth and a storage room just behind it. Oh, yes, another such form had been seen in the former concession booth area of the the theater.

All of these entities are believed to be one and the same–the spirit of the founder of the theater, Mr. Hersker.

Wherever and whenever his energy manifests itself, nothing untoward happens. It seems as if old Mr. Hersker is simply keeping an eternal eye over his films, equipment, theater, and those who attend movies or events there.

It is well known in ghost-hunting circles that extensive renovations of a building can "stir up," so to speak, resident energies. With all the renovations through all of the years in the Key/Hersker/Cinema & Drafthouse, it is entirely likely that Mr. Hersker's spirit may still dwell there and make an occasional appearance.

Tales from Lake Winola:
THE LADY OF THE LAKE
AND THE
CAMPGROUND PHANTOM

Does the ghost of a forlorn Indian maiden continue to haunt the waters, shore, and land around Lake Winola?

It would be the ghost of Winola herself, the star-crossed and ill-fated daughter of the powerful Minsi Chief Capouse.

Winola lived with her father on the banks of the lake that now bears her name. A young and desirable woman, Winola attracted the attention of one young man with whom she would rendezvous not far from her father's lakeside home. Their meetings had to remain a secret, however, as Chief Capouse had made it clear that he did not approve of the young brave.

It is said that one bright morning, Winola went to the edge of the lake to gather water. The surface of the lake was mirror smooth. And, to her shock and surprise, in that mirror-like water she saw the reflection of her mighty father, carrying the scalp of her lover. Distressed and confused, she dove into the lake, disappeared deep within it, and returned only as a spirit that remains there to this day.

Sightings of her ghost have been reported on and around Lake Winola for generations.

And, while the owners of the Highland Campgrounds, a couple miles south of Lake Winola on Old Mill Drive, do not attempt to link the "Lady of the Lake" with the unexplainable occurrences within their 35-acre facility, it could well be that her spirit may have a hand in them.

"The first stirrings we noticed were in the first year we had the campground," said Nancy Mayer. "When we first took it over, I felt something wasn't right. To be in the one end of the camp by myself would make the hair rise on the back of my neck.

"Even to drive through at night made me uncomfortable. I mentioned this to some of my seasonal campers at that end of the camp and they mentioned to me what they had observed."

Nancy explained that there was not a threatening or evil sense to any of it, but just an overriding sense of foreboding.

"We had two seasonal sites that seemed to have activity," she added. That activity ranged from camper doors opening and closing with no human aid and a strange mist rising and floating in the area of those two sites.

"Also in the first year," she continued, "we had an overnight guest come to the office wanting to know why the ground under her camper was 'shaking.' My husband didn't know what to think, but said he'd be down to check. When he got down there, the shaking stopped. We thought that she maybe was a bit 'off' but kept that in the back of our minds due to the other events that had taken place.

"That fall, we had the camp logged out. After the loggers left, it was our responsibility to clean up the tree tops that were left behind. We were working together in the upper area of the camp removing tops and brush when my daughter Sara said, 'Hey mom, the ground is shaking.' I stepped over near her and it indeed was moving. I could feel a deep rhythmic vibration through my boots. My husband was busy cutting with the chain saw. I didn't want to yell to him for fear he might get hurt. Unfortunately, when he finished, the vibration went away."

Her natural inclination was to believe the vibration was still just from his cutting. "I remained in place and he resumed cutting, but the movement did not return. Now, you have to realize this is in January, so all the power had been shut off and the water had been shut off for the season. It really got my interest going. I even went so far as to see if there were any 'faults' mapped on the area in which the camp stood–nothing."

Nancy also noted that, to her knowledge,

there are no mine shafts beneath the campground.

"So again," she shrugged, "we took it in stride and filed it away in out minds, thinking, okay, so maybe that woman wasn't so 'off.'"

Other campers have subsequently reported strange shaking sensations in certain areas of the campgrounds. Nancy confirmed that there have been no known earthquakes there, and there are no mine shafts beneath the grounds.

Mysterious mists and queer quaking aside, the sightings by other campers may be the most awesome of all events at the otherwise tranquil and hospitable Highland Campgrounds.

"Last year," Nancy said, "we had guests who told us that at about three in the morning they decided to go walking down an unfinished path. They told us they had seen images of Indians and men in uniform, fighting in the woods!"

What part of the campgrounds is "enchanted?" On what trail might you catch a glimpse of the phantom soldiers and Indians? Nancy left those questions unanswered, fodder for the inquiring and imaginative guests who might just add their own experiences to the ever-expanding annals of the unexplainable there.

THE SUSCON SCREAMER

We first examined the story of the "Suscon Screamer" in our 1995 book *Pocono Ghosts, Legends & Lore: Book Two*.

The story remains as one of the most enduring legends (or...is it just a legend?) in Luzerne County and warrants another look in this volume.

Set in a hilly, rocky, remote section just east of Suscon, the tale incorporates several elements of a classic "urban legend." But, it also includes features that make it stand alone and beg for belief.

The centerpiece of the story was the "Black Bridge" in Jenkins Township. Some called it the "Boo-Boo" or "Beep-Beep" Bridge, as it was so narrow that only one car could pass at a time. As drivers approached it, they were advised to slow down or stop and honk *(Boo-Boo, Beep-Beep)* their horns to warn opposing motorists.

That, it was said, could literally wake the dead!

The horn honking could well be followed by the appearance of a young woman in a white dress who would emerge from the darkness and fade away under the bridge. On occasion, she would let out a muffled scream...hence, the "Suscon

Screamer."

It was said that it was the ghost of a girl who had been murdered near the bridge. One version is that she was a newlywed who was leaving her wedding with her new husband when their car broke down in the wee, small hours of the morning at the Black Bridge. Her husband told her to stay put in the car while he sought help. When he returned to the car, she was in the back seat, dead.

That led to another version of the story, in which motorists approaching the bridge would see in their rearview mirror the pallid face of an anguished young woman. She would appear mysteriously and suddenly, and as soon as the driver would turn around to look at her, she would vanish.

Still another explanation is that the ghost is that of a young *would-be* bride who was jilted at the altar and ran into the woods to the bridge, where she hanged herself.

And then, there's the possibility that the young woman is a high school girl who was killed on her prom night.

One thing all of these stories have in common is that the forlorn female phantom will, if conditions are right, utter a scream and validate the legend.

Oh, did I mention the element in which that

stretch of the Suscon Road near the old bridge is a "gravity hill" where, if you put your car into neutral at one point, that car will coast *up* the grade? Some have attributed that to the powerful energies that have been imprinted there by...whomever.

There are those in the area who will swear by their experiences there, and others who will scoff at them. However, every legend has its root in fact.

It is a fact that on October 4, 1969, two men were walking along the Suscon Road near the Black Bridge when they made a grisly discovery.

The corpse of a 15-year old Avoca girl lay in the leaves just off the side of the road. She had been hitchhiking and got a ride from a 26-year old man who was soon captured and convicted of her murder. In 2000, while serving a life sentence at the state prison in Graterford, the murderer died.

The victim was not a newlywed. She was not wearing white. But could it be that the final, frantic moments of her life can still be heard down at the Black Bridge? Could she be...the Suscon Screamer?

Into the Light...

It is a typical residence in West Hazleton that has been home to several generations of the same family.

It is a pleasant, comfortable place...now.

But, for more than three years, the restless ramblings of two spirits wreaked havoc in the life of one woman and rippled into the lives of those who lived with her.

The address of the property and the names of those who dealt with the situation will not be divulged, as per their request.

Follow the cast of characters closely, and stay with the story until the end, when a possible explanation for the haunting will be offered.

It is a classic tale of one individual beset by what she truly believed were vexing visitors and a family support system comprised of believers and skeptics. In the end, however, the believers seemed to prevail.

An elderly woman lived alone in an apartment on the second floor of the building. Her son and daughter-in-law resided in the downstairs apartment.

It was the woman upstairs who said that she was being tormented by mysterious beings.

"She would often stand at the top of the steps and say *'Tell them to go away!'*," the daughter-in-law said. "She told us that they wouldn't leave her alone, that she couldn't sleep."

The old woman was so affected by the ghosts that she would leave her lights on at night in an effort to keep them away.

As she was up in age, her rants were initially dismissed as those of someone possibly in the first stages of dementia. But, those around her knew better. These were genuine fears.

Just who "they" were–just who plagued the woman for more than three years–could never positively be determined. But, some family members believed they knew.

"I think there were two of them," the woman's daughter-in-law said. She believed that the old woman's mother-in-law and first husband were the restless energies that ambled and gamboled in the upstairs apartment.

Another of the old woman's daughters-in-laws agreed that there were two spirits that visited her. She lived out of town, but would be enrobed in the experience whenever she visited.

"She was a nervous wreck," that second daughter-in-law agreed.

"Whenever she would tell me to tell them (the entities) to go away, I would actually shout to them to *'Go to the light! Go to the light!'*."

Everyone in the extended family did their best to assuage the woman's anxieties. But, she continued to believe with all her heart, mind, and soul that she was being haunted.

The upstairs ghosts were invisible and undetectable to anyone other than the old woman, but there were certain incidents in the downstairs apartment that caused her kin to believe that something might be awry.

The daughter-in-law who lived on the first floor apartment was constantly annoyed with candles that she lit in the early evening, snuffed at the end of the evening, but were later re-lit by unseen hands. After that happened one or two times, she would take extra and careful note that she blew out the candle, and it was truly out. Cold...not lit...out!

Voila! The candle would flicker, flare, and flame!

But what would be of most interest to anyone who has studied such stories are the reports of a closet door that would just not stay closed.

Again, special care would be taken to ensure that the closet door was closed. Clunk...latched...shut!

Voila! The closet door would unclunk, unlatch, and open!

As it turns out, that was not always a closet door.

At one time, that door opened to steps that led down and into the cellar. During extensive renovations to the building, those steps were removed and a closet was built inside what was the old cellar door.

It was through that door and down those steps that the husband of the hexed old woman would escape into his downstairs workshop where he spent hours tinkering on various and sundry projects. It was his special place.

And, the gent also spent hours in his favorite chair, which was situated in close proximity to the old cellar door.

It was in that chair that he died.

And, all of that information could be vital to speculating about the identity of one of the spirits in the building.

The removal of the cellar steps and the sealing of the space to create a closet may very well have altered the "flow" of the residual energy of the man who so often used those steps–and who passed on so close to them. It may have caused the various anomalies in the environment inside the apartments.

That same basic scenario has been played out in numerous buildings where ghostly activity is reported. Adding or removing walls, reconfiguring spaces, and interrupting that passage of energy seems to be common contributors to a haunting.

But, was the old woman upstairs merely fighting personal demons? No one in the family can be certain, and it is not for this writer to judge.

"But," said the daughter-in-law who lived in the building and bore the brunt of the uneasiness, "ever since she passed away, things have been quiet. The door stays closed, the candles stay lit, and all is well."

Hopefully, those rambunctious wraiths–and presumably the woman in the upstairs apartment–indeed followed and found "the light."

FACELESS PHANTOMS IN FORTY FORT

By her own admission, she is a Christian, he a "believer in God and in Heaven." In a letter to me, she further described herself as married and the mother of three children.

But, she has lived her life with a deep and possibly dark memory lurking beneath that veneer of contentment.

She was raised in Forty Fort, not far from the cemetery and the Susquehanna. For the purposes of this publication, I shall call her Jane. And, I will let her words tell the story.

"When I was approximately ten or 11 years old," Jane said, "I was walking along Wyoming Avenue with my younger sister.

"I noticed two people walking toward us, but on the other side of the street. It was an summer evening, and about to get dark.

"What made me look at them was the fact that they were dressed alike. They looked like people without faces, hands, or ankles. They walked along the cemetery fence on the sidewalk in our direction. Their clothes were white, and one was taller than the other by about a foot or maybe two.

"At the moment I saw them, I stopped

walking and told my younger sister to look at them because they looked so different and strange.

"I could see no faces, hair, necks, hands, or ankles. Almost at the same time that I saw them and stopped to stare and point at them, they immediately turned toward the dark cemetery and they appeared to leap through the iron fence into the cemetery and disappear!"

Both girls were stunned. They scurried across the street and looked inside the cemetery fence. They saw and heard nothing.

"I will never forget how they turned at the same time and jumped, leaping through the air like a deer. They went through the iron fence and vanished before touching the ground."

Jane has had other encounters with the unexplainable over her lifetime, but those one or two minutes on that busy avenue so long ago will never be purged from her memory–if she can help it.

"To this day," Jane continued, "my sister will not speak of what we saw that evening. She only acknowledges that it happened, and that is all. While I tell everyone about it so that I will never forget it.

"I know that as people age, their memories may fade. But I will never, ever forget what happened that night at that cemetery."

A vintage view of the Conyngham Hotel/Brass Buckle

THE BRASS BUCKLE

...OF GUACAMOLE AND GHOSTS!

I had a hunch. As my research assistant and I canvassed Conyngham for possible supernatural sites, the old Conyngham Hotel drew me in like a paranormal magnet.

I did not let the fact that the old hotel has been a Mexican restaurant deter me. After all, Mexican restaurants can have ghosts. And, the likely ghost of the former hotel has been lingering there long before the chimichangas came to call.

There is evidence that the first tavern at what is now 334 Main Street was built around 1812. It

129

was, of course, greatly enlarged and modified over the next century, and through those years was a popular gathering spot for townsfolk. In the 1950s and '60s, the building served as a nursing home.

Despite certain modernizations and modifications, the building is still recognizable as one of those quintessential country hotels.

I was attracted to the Brass Buckle because I felt there was a story there–a ghost story.

I couldn't have visited at a more opportune time. It was the Halloween season, and from the entrance to the restaurant to the farthest reaches of the dining rooms, imaginative and expressive spooky decorations turned the place into a veritable theme park of creepiness. Creepiness by design, that is.

But, as I waited for someone to speak with, I discovered that there was no need to invent a eerie atmosphere. There is a resident ghost there.

I was greeted by Allen Hildebrand, who knows the old hotel building as well as anyone. He lived there for ten years, on the first and second floors. He's worked at the restaurant for nearly 20 years, and he takes great pride in the business and the building.

I played the role of the inquisitive reporter at first, asking if there were any spirits within the walls of the place.

He proceeded to speak of the random

opening and closing of doors and other assorted incidents that led workers there to think a ghost may be afoot.

As he was talking, I was distracted by what I felt was a very strong energy in one particular section of the restaurant.

It was a wall, just inside the restaurant, at the doors to the rest rooms.

I listened to Allen with one sense and drank in the ethereal energies with another.

He continued his stories. "We had a night of conversation here about a man, George Drumheller, who owned the building in the early 1900s. In 1907, there was a fire on the opposite side of the street. It had spread, claiming several structures.

"The story is that Drumheller had walked out on the front porch of the hotel and saw the fire. Concerned that it might spread further and consume his hotel, he had a heart attack and dropped over dead at the front door on the front porch."

Mr. Drumheller's ill fate has been generally regarded as what left a ghostly imprint on the building.

"One time, I was telling that story to some folks here," Allen continued. "I said that I wished I knew if there was a presence here, or not. And, just as I said that, a mirror that had been glued to the wall for 30-some years fell on the floor and smashed.

"Honestly, I ran out of here like a bat out of hell!"

That mirror was on the wall, just inside the restaurant, at the doors to the rest rooms.

As Allen was telling his story about telling his story, I chafed at the bit to tell my story.

All along, I had been sensing a very strong presence just over my shoulder, on that wall at the doors to the rest rooms. In fact, it seemed to me that there was a shaft of energy that extended within that wall and up through the basement ceiling to whatever was above that wall.

My sensation and his story dovetailed exquisitely. And, I had that sensation well before he told the story of Mr. Drumheller.

It was on that wall that I felt the strong energy, and it was on that wall from which the mirror tumbled, giving Allen and others a sign that the presence was present.

Giving it all a bit more thought, Allen came to an unsettling realization. That wall, and the reconfigured space behind it, was just under what had been the main steps to the front porch and front door–at what was almost certainly the spot where George Drumheller suffered his fatal heart attack, and is the epicenter of the haunting.

🜚

Eliza's Ghost:
Guarding the Gold?

The ruins of "The Good Place" on the Briggs Farm, ca. 1928. (From a Berwick Enterprise *clipping)*

This tale is the very embodiment of this book. It is almost equal parts ghost story, legend, and lore.

The setting is grim and gloomy. The plot is the incessant search for an alleged horde of gold that is hidden somewhere within its ruins. The central character is a woman–and perhaps a ghost–named Eliza.

A handsome homestead when it was built in 1832 on the sprawling lands of the Briggs family, namesakes of Briggsville, what has long been known as "The Good Place" has been reduced to rubble since it was abandoned in the late 19th century.

It is situated in an isolated section of the 350-acre spread still owned and farmed by the Briggs family. What is left of the Good Place is barely recognizable as the sturdy fieldstone building it once was.

"It has always been strange to me as to why that particular house and outbuildings were abandoned," said Richard Briggs. "It's not like the rest of the family moved away. There were brothers and sisters who lived within walking distance, right on the farm. So, it remains a mystery to me why it was left to go to ruin."

Perhaps it has something to do with the enigmatic uttering of its last resident.

Briggs may wonder why it was ever abandoned, but he has a good sense about why it steadily wasted away to ruin–with a lot of help.

"From the time I was little," Briggs said, "I know that people have gone through it because of what Eliza Good said on her deathbed."

And what did she say? What led generation after generation of ransackers and rogues to the

Good Place?

The story of what Eliza Good said just before she died has been circulating up Nescopeck way for more than a century.

We turn to the pages of the *Berwick Enterprise* of December 22, 1932.

According to legend of the countryside, the old Good home holds a treasure in money, the ghostly heritage of Eliza Briggs Good:

Old wives' tales relate that Mrs. Good secreted her wealth somewhere within the massive stone walls of the ancient house. Later owners and adventurers alike have searched in every nook and cranny in search of the reputed treasure, but to no avail. The limestone walls refuse to reveal the secret to their treasure chest.

Were these just "old wives' tales?" Richard Briggs wasn't quick to pass judgment. But, he did admit that others' quest for the booty has led to the downfall of the old place.

"People pulled the stones out," he said, "and pulled the house down looking for it."

And, in that 1932 newspaper article, the rapid decline and fall of the house was lamented:

All about the place is a feeling of awe and desolation. Perhaps the spirits of Peter Good and his wife, Eliza, guard the secrets of their earthly home; perhaps its gloomy location on the edge of a swamp lends fear to its sombre loneliness; perhaps the superstition of the neighborhood makes it a place to be avoided by cautious folk.

The windowpanes have long since disappeared but the weatherbeaten frames remain in the yellowed walls like the shrunken eyes of a corpse.

It looks as bleak and disconsolate as the dreary house of usher in Poe's famed story.

Poe? Spirits? Superstition? Now, we venture into another realm regarding the old ruins.

Is the Good Place a bad place, in a ghostly sense? Has Eliza's eternal energy been lurking there, luring the prospectors onto the property and leaving them in the lurch?

In 1890, Eliza Briggs Good suffered a stroke and died at the age of 86.

As she lay dying, Eliza is said to have told family members that as they entered her room they passed the hiding place of her fortune.

That revelation piqued the curiosity of all who heard it or heard about it. Not long after the old woman's heart stop beating did the fall of the house of Good commence.

Rumors of Eliza's ghost, and perhaps even Peter's spirit inhabiting their desolate and desecrated old home have spread through the region for years.

Richard Briggs confided that he has never actually witnessed an apparition there, or anywhere on the land that is still farmed by his father and two sons. But, the television producer and promoter of the annual Briggs Farm Blues Festival does sense those who came before him.

"We are very close to our ancestors here," he said. "The farm has never belonged to anyone else. We're living on their footprints. I have always felt the presence of my ancestors here."

Of what is still called "The Good Place," even in its shameful state, Briggs is cautious. "It has a very eerie feeling to it. I don't know if it's just because it's in ruins, but I would not be out there alone at night."

And, of the possibility–however remote–that a cache of gold is still buried somewhere in the remains of the house? "We've never made any concerted effort to find the gold," he said. "Who knows? It's possible that someone already did find it and didn't tell us, or anyone else, about it!"

There is yet another tempting tidbit to this story that may add yet another dimension to its intrigue.

Recent archaeological digs at the Good Place revealed no precious metals, but did unearth the foundations of earlier structures and relics from what is believed to be an Indian settlement that thrived on the site 3,000 years ago.

While yet a boy I sought for ghosts, and sped
Through many a listening chamber,
cave and ruin,
And starlight wood, with fearful steps pursuing
Hopes of high talk with the departed dead.

Percy Bysshe Shelley

Part Two
LEGENDS

BLOODY ROCK

THE SHADES OF DEATH

and

The Fiend of the Susquehanna

Bloody Rock...then.

The early history of the Wyoming Valley is drenched with the blood of the settlers who fell to the barbaric natives determined to protect their land.

It is difficult today to imagine the lay of the land then. While the valleys of the Susquehanna afforded rich soil for farming, there were areas in this corner of Penn's Woods that were deep, dark, and foreboding.

It was also a cauldron of political controversy. It is now, of course, firmly locked in the Commonwealth of Pennsylvania. And, in the 17th century it seemed to be within the bounds of William Penn's family grant. However, another grant overseen by the governor of Connecticut claimed the same land. So, before any battles with natives and any battles with the British, there were territorial disputes between two colonies. At one point, virtually everything now known as Pennsylvania's Wyoming Valley was part of Litchfield County, Connecticut. Strange, indeed.

As more and more settlers and investors ventured into the valley, those disputes erupted into what history records as the "Yankee-Pennamite Wars."

In the years just prior to the Revolutionary War, skirmishes and outright battles between the Yankees (Connecticut) and the Pennamites (Pennsylvanians) resulted a most *unsettling* atmosphere among the settlers.

Just as those troubles were being resolved, to a degree, another challenge came to the valley.

It is recorded in history as the Revolutionary War.

Only a relative handful of Colonial militia men were garrisoned in the area, and invading British troops and their Indian allies stormed the virtually defenseless forts along the Susquehanna and in one day, July 3, 1778, virtually annihilated the defenders.

It is recorded in history as the Battle of Wyoming.

This is not a history book, but it is from that battle, or probably more properly, "massacre" that several legends have taken root.

One is the "Shades of Death," a course taken by settlers who escaped the attack on July 3. Seeking salvation, they fled through the "Great Swamp" of Buck Township. Although they may have saved themselves from the massacre, many are said to have died miserable deaths in the thick forests and swamp lands there.

In his 1858 book, "Wyoming: Its History, Stirring Incidents, and Romantic Adventures," author George Peck painted a grisly picture of the aftermath of the short but savage battle:

Nearly all the settlers in the valley perished; for the few troops left at home, mostly old men and boys, were no match for the sudden onslaught of the fierce, crafty, weather-hardened Indians and the even more savage Tories. The entire valley was for a time at the mercy of these dastards.

142

Helpless children and women were tortured, tomahawked, and treated in every conceivable beastly manner. The hapless captives were shown no mercy.

Perhaps the most ominous of all remnants of the Wyoming Massacre is what is "officially" known as Queen Esther's Rock, on Susquehanna Avenue near 7th Street in Wyoming.

Queen Esther, or Esther Montour, was the product of mixed Indian-white marriages in what is now New York State.

Referred to by one historian as "the fiend of the Susquehanna," Esther is said to have been enraged by the killing of her son, Andrew, in Exeter on July 2, 1778 and vowed revenge.

That revenge came two days later when Esther was apprised of 16 white settlers who had been captured and detained along the river.

Legend has it that she hastened to the site and ordered the doomed men around a boulder and, one by one, smashed their skulls with a tomahawk. Or, as Peck described it:

The prisoners were seated upon the rock, held by two strong Indians, while the priestess of the bloody rites which were performed upon that fatal altar chanted a savage dirge or war-song, and raising the death-mall with both hands, dashed out the brains of the helpless victim, or with one hand buried her hatchet in his skull.

143

Bloody Rock, a.k.a.
"Queen Esther's Rock"

To this day, "Bloody Rock" remains. In 1896, the Wyoming Valley Chapter of the Daughters of the American Revolution erected a historical marker there and protected the rock with a steel grate. It had been severely damaged by relic hunters throughout the 19th century.

The rock is located in the middle of a mixed commercial/residential block of Susquehanna Avenue near 7th Street in Wyoming. The D.A.R. plaque has been supplemented by a state historical marker. An iron fence surrounds the small site.

TOBY'S CAVE

The outcropping of rocks known as Toby's Cave, near the mouth of Toby's Creek, holds within it an eerie legend or two.

Said to once be the hermitage of an Indian named Toby (for whom the creek was named), the cave was also reported to be haunted.

Believed by some to be nearly a mile long, the cave was a place to be avoided because of the spirits that supposedly dwelled inside it.

Over the years, several tales of moaning sounds and eerie, glowing figures gathering at the entrance of the cave led some to think that they were the ghosts of early settlers who found refuge from the early Indian warfare, only to perish from exposure and/or starvation inside the cave.

THE LOST SISTER

It is a story that spans three centuries and several states. Its drama has left its mark forever in history books and maps. It is the story of a woman who has a playground, a state park, a state recreation area, two hiking trails in two states, a college residence hall, a cemetery, a town, and even a bank named after her.

146

Frances Slocum is spirited away by the Indians.

It is the story of Frances Slocum.

Or, is it the story of Mocanaquah?

It is the story of both, as they are one in the same.

The story began on November 2, 1778, when hostilities between settlers and Indians were running hot in the Wyoming Valley.

Frances was about five years old when a band of Indians swooped down on the humble house of her Quaker parents in what is now Wilkes-Barre.

Her father, Jonathan, was a fair distance from the house, working the land with two of his sons, Giles and William.

At the house were Frances, Mary, Ebenezer, Joseph, and the infant Jonathan Slocum and

Frances Slocum/Mocanaquah

their mother, Ruth. Also there were Wareham and Nathan Kingsley, who had come to stay with the Slocums after their father was kidnapped by the Indians.

Wielding tomahawks and muskets, Delaware Indian Chief Tuck Horse led the raiders into the house.

Nathan Kingsley was the first to fall, shot dead. His brother was abducted by an Indian, and in the melee Mary took her baby brother Jonathan and ran into the woods. Joseph Slocum escaped and ran toward Fort Wyoming to get help.

148

Meanwhile, Frances and Ebenezer had gone into the house and hidden under a staircase.

It is said that Tuck Horse himself found the children cringing in fear. It is also said that he was taken by her striking auburn hair and that she reminded him of the deceased daughter of a friend.

Ruth Slocum watched in horror as the Indians carried out their assault.

In later years, Frances Slocum recalled the horrid events of the day:

"I can well remember the day when the Delaware Indians came suddenly to our house," she is quoted in John F. Meginness's 1891 *Biography of Frances Slocum.*

"I remember that they killed and scalped a man near the door, taking the scalp with them. They then pushed the boy through the door, he came to me and we both went and hid under the staircase. They went upstairs and rifled the house, though I cannot remember what they took. I remember that they took me and the boy on their backs through the bushes. I believe the rest of the family had fled, except my mother."

Indeed, Ruth Slocum's life was spared. But, she had been traumatized as her home and family were destroyed that day. About a month later, her husband was also shot and scalped by the Indians.

Meanwhile, the kidnapped Frances Slocum was taken on a journey that can truly be called "life changing."

The Indian chief was protective of his captive. Again from the Meginness book, "They carried us a long way," Frances recalled, "to a cave where they had left their blankets and traveling things. It was over the mountain and a long way down on the other side. Here they stopped while it was yet light, and there we stayed all night. I can remember nothing about that night, except that I was very tired and lay down on the ground and cried till I was asleep."

From that rocky shelter, Frances was swept into a new world–the world of the Indians.

Her captors traveled long and far west, eventually to Indiana. There, they settled. Frances had been indoctrinated into their ways, and back in Wilkes-Barre, all hope that she might still be alive had been dashed.

Through a series of uncanny events, however, she was found alive and well in an Indian Village near Peru, Indiana–some 57 years after her kidnapping!

An Indian Agent named Col. George W. Ewing was introduced to an Indian woman named Mocanaquah, or "little bear." He suspected that she may not have been a full-blooded Indian. He engaged her in conversation, and although she had by now spoken only broken English (contrary, of course, to Meginness's alleged quotes mentioned earlier) and remembered only scant details of her brief childhood in the Wyoming Valley, she made it clear that she had been taken from a house in Pennsylvania and had become inculcated with the Indian way of life.

Col. Ewing wrote her story and sent it in a letter to the postmaster of Lancaster, Pa. The postmaster there found it to be an interesting story, but could offer little help. Two years later, the letter was published in a newspaper and the story made its way to Wilkes-Barre where, incredibly, it was read by long-lost friends and family members.

Several of them journeyed to Indiana in an attempt to "rescue" Mocanaquah.

They found that she was quite content, and had totally adopted and embraced the Indian lifestyle. She had her own extended family, and had no intention or inclination to return to Pennsylvania or abandon her new family.

Frances Slocum had essentially passed away the day she was taken away from her white family's home.

Mocanaquah died on Marcy 9, 1847 near Reserve, Indiana. She is buried beneath a stately monument on the banks of the Mississinewa River.

The "cave" in which little Frances spent her first night as a prisoner of the Indians is accessible on the trail and in the state park that both bear Frances Slocum's name.

As you hike there and stand beneath its broad stone canopy, imagine the sheer terror and sense of uncertainty that little girl felt that night. And, listen...it is said that to this day, the faint, ghostly cries of Frances Slocum can be heard echoing eternally.

Frances Slocum has been remembered in monuments, playgrounds, schools, books, parks, and even a bank

FRANCES SLOCUM ELEMENTARY

FRANCES SLOCUM
Captured as a child by the Delaware Indians in 1778 from her Pennsylvania home, she grew up with the Indians, married a Miami chief, and lived in Indiana till her death. 1847

Frances Slocum Bank
your partners in success

MACONAQUAH'S STORY
THE SAGA OF FRANCES SLOCUM
BY KITTY DYE

MONUMENT TO FRANCES SLOCUM, the "White

A LUZERNE COUNTY VILLAGE NAMED AFTER A MURDER?

It is generally believed these days that Wapwallopen derived its name from the natives' designation of "where the white hemp grows."

Perhaps.

However, in his 1899 book "Down the Historic Susquehanna: A Summer's Jaunt from Otsego to the Chesapeake," author Charles Weathers Bump published an entirely different explanation of the name.

His description of the local landscape was eloquent:

At Shickshinny the river makes a sharp turn south, and so continues for six miles to Wapwallopen, where it again swerves westward. The left bank for this six miles is closely bounded by the Wapwallopen hill, which terminates above the village of Wapwallopen in a vigorous and grand rocky front, 900 feet high, known as "Pulpit Rock"-"Kansal Kopf" it was called by some German pioneers. It is a fine outlook, for the mountains diminish below Wapwallopen, and the remainder of our journey was through a rich agricultural region; with hills, it is true, but neither high nor steep, and set back in a way to invite farmers to the intervales.

And then, he offered an explanation for the name of the village at the foot of the hill of the same name:

Wapwallopen means "where the messenger was murdered," and is said to have been first applied after the killing of Thomas Hill, a messenger to Wyoming from the Governor of Pennsylvania. It is chiefly of interest as the site of big powder mills, operated for the last 40 years by the Du Ponts. of Wilmington.

IS THERE SILVER IN THEM THAR HILLS?

What's more, in his book, Bump fudged with the naming of Campbell's Ledge–a "bold mountain" with a "rocky, scowling summit"–but did allude to its alleged ancient celestial significance:

The old inhabitants called the ledge Dial Knob because the exact location of its

*face north and south enabled noon to be
told miles away on a sunlit day.*

He also repeated an oft-told tale that spoke of a mineral more precious that coal that might be found at Campbell's Ledge:

*It has been handed down from father to
son for the last century or more that away
in the deep recesses of some glade of
Campbell's Ledge is a silver mine of incom-
putable wealth that was known and
operated by the aborigines.*

Another version of that same story claimed there was a deep vein of gold, not silver, somewhere in the innards of Campbell's Ledge.

Campbell's Ledge from Peck's "Wyoming."

THE WITCH
OF BLACK CREEK

These days, the locals call it "Tank." In olden days, those who traversed that area of bucolic Black Creek Township "cursed."

The story of "The Witch of Black Creek" has largely faded into the darkest recesses of Luzerne County history, but could the presence of the "black-eyed, raven-haired witch" who prowled the road through the gap two centuries ago still be there?

That gap was described in an 1880 article in the *Lebanon Daily Times* as–with apologies to Black Creek Township residents–"one of the most dismal places to be found in the country." The story continued:

Only a narrow stretch of sky is visible from below, and this is almost always filled with a haze, which the sunbeams scarcely ever penetrate. When the sky happens to be clear there is no sunrise in the gap until 10 o'clock, while at two the sun goes down. Immense gray boulders abound. The ground is covered with the ashes and trunks of fallen pines, charred and blacked by mountain fires, which yearly sweep over the place, lie decaying, sometimes one across the other. Enormous snakes crawl over the rocks or bathe in the slimy pools. The only trees are stunted pines, which grow out from between the rocks.

Hmm...decaying trees, enormous snakes, slimy pools. Remember, dear reader, that those are not my words.

But, they are words that paint a classic backdrop for a legend or two.

In addition to the gloom and desolation infesting the place, it has, according to the people thereabouts, been sadly troubled with witches.

The author of the original story confessed that at one time, presumably around 1800, that very same gap was a wondrous place with green forests that blossomed under blue skies. Birds sang and wildlife was plentiful.

So abundant was the fauna of the gap that hunters were drawn to it like steel to a magnet.

But, it was an incident involving those hunters that led to the gap's late-19th century reputation as being cursed.

It seems that a group of hunters was in the woods when two shots rang out and one big buck fell.

Two of the marksmen claimed the kill, and in an ensuing fight, one of the hunters was mortally wounded.

As word of the incident spread through the region, the dead man's sister found her way to the hunting cabin in the gap and accosted her brother's slayer. She was the aforementioned "black-eyed, raven-haired" woman, and she is the one who was responsible for flipping the fortunes of the gap.

As she cradled the body of her brother in her arms, she issued a blasphemous curse on the man who dealt the fatal blow. Her curse resonated throughout the gap.

In a short time the waters of the creek became black and sulphurous, the sky grew dim and hazy, while the gap became the abode of serpents and a scene of desolation.

And, the gap became the lair of what became known as "The Witch of Black Creek."

She never left the tight valley, and was feared by all who navigated the narrows.

The black-eyed girl was frequently seen–sometimes walking through the gap at midnight, enveloped in a large black cloak; at other times in the midst of the tempest, on the top of the loftiest tree, swaying to and fro, with her long black hair streaming in the wind.

The witch also made herself known by stopping horses dead in their tracks, bogging down wagons traversing the gap, and dooming nearby enterprises to failure.

The whole place has become the abode of wretchedness and misery.

And that's the way it was...in Black Creek Township, Luzerne County, circa 1880.

Pookas and Banshees in Archbald?

Should you ever find yourself in Ireland, be aware of the creepy creatures they call pookas, banshees, faeries, leprechauns, and goblins!

Should you ever find yourself in Archbald, be on guard for the presence of the very same legendary beings.

When immigrants from across the British Isles and Europe settled in Northeastern Pennsylvania, they brought with them their quaint customs and beliefs.

Some of those beliefs dabbled in the "dark side" of life...and the afterlife.

As Irish immigrants came to Archbald, their

ominous omens came along for the ride. They included the banshee and the pooka.

Depending on your tolerance for such beasts, the banshee is probably the one you'd fear the most. Appearing as a raggedy hag that soars and shrieks in the night as a portent of an impending death, this figure was apparently a fixture in Archbald "back in the day."

In his 1916 book "Old Time Archbald," writer D.J. Gilmartin detailed the doings of both the banshees and the pookas in the hills around the town.

Pookas were powerful apparitions, usually ink-black horses with glowing yellow eyes, that reared up and ruined crops, outbuildings, and nervous systems of rural residents and farmers. They could also shift their shape to become fanged rabbits, glowing foxes, or whatever they believed could do the most physical and psychological damage.

Were these merely legends of long ago that have been relegated to the fragile pages of an ancient tome?

Perhaps.

But, should you find yourself in Archbald, be aware....be very aware...of the pooka and the banshee!

The
Witch
Tree
and
the
Death
Couch

Two Luzerne County legends that are likely to never go away are those of the "Witch Tree" near Drifton and the "Death Couch" near Eckley.

The stories have passed the test of time and continue to fascinate generation after generation of those who tell or are told.

Ask three people in the area about the tree or the couch and you'll get as many versions of the stories.

But, one thing has been constant...severe consequences *could* befall those who tempt the evil spirits that are said to congregate around or within both the tree and the couch.

Try as I may have, and having asked a half-dozen people around Drifton and Freeland where the "Witch Tree" (or, as one wag referred to it, the "Devil's Tree") I found nothing that resembled what most described.

It is, so the story goes, the mangled remains of a tree that was smashed into by a car of teenagers out for a joy ride one night. The ride proved to be their last. Their car careened off the road and into the tree, killing all two, three, or four of them, again depending on the teller of the tale.

What is agreed is that when the tree healed its wounds, the hideous form of the face of a deformed witch grew on its gnarled trunk.

It is said that the Witch Tree has taken on powers that actually attempt to lure unsuspecting motorists into its deformed trunk. And, should anyone even *touch* that tree, it is further said, he or she will meet the same fate as those unfortunate teens.

According to a consensus of those asked, the

LUZERNE AND LACKAWANNA COUNTIES GHOSTS

tree is supposedly located along St. Ann's Drive near Drifton.

The "Death Couch," or, variously, the "Haunted Couch" or "Stone Couch" is another leathery legend from Foster Township.

It is a rock formation that uncannily resembles a couch. Situated along Buck Mountain Road a mile or so south of Eckley Miners' Village, the "couch" has been a staple of local lore for decades.

Whether the victims died in a carriage or car accident, by infanticide/suicide, or a double murder, it is said that a woman and her baby were killed at that precise spot, and their anguished energies remain there, using the "couch" as a convenient lure for their evildoings.

The unique and inviting shape of the outcropping of rocks has led many to its "seat." And, sitting in it could lead the daring (or dumb) to their deaths.

As the story goes, if you sit on the couch one time, bad luck will befall you. If you sit in it twice, someone you know will die. If you sit in it three time, *you* will die!

Many a tale has been told of those who have teased their fates by sitting on the couch once and having almost immediate bad luck. They would never go back for a second seating.

Pictures allegedly showing the misty forms

of the ghosts of the woman and her child have been taken there. And, two individuals from nearby Freeland told me that they have caught fleeting glimpses of the ghosts of the mother and baby standing in the middle of Buck Mountain Road as if to dare them to drive into them. As they hit the brakes to avoid hitting the phantoms, they vanish!

One legend-busting old-timer in the area said he had documented proof that the "couch" was actually crafted by Depression-era Works Progress Administration (WPA) workers who made it with leftover concrete from a road project.

And, there are those who say the entire matter is the stuff of pure urban legend. They have lounged on the stony sofa several times, without incident.

Very well.

Find the couch.

Sit on it.

See what happens.

Sit on it again.

And again.

I dare you.

Is it nothing but an urban legend after all?

Let me know—or, have your next of kin let me know!

THE LEGEND COLLECTOR

I would never have thought to compile a collection of ghost stories, legends, and lore of Luzerne and Lackawanna counties without first contacting Dr. William Ellis, professor of English at Penn State Hazleton.

He is himself a legend as a collector of contemporary folklore, urban legends, and all things supernatural.

Dr. Ellis soars high in the aerie of academia, while this humble writer flaps and flutters in the breezes of "popular" literature.

But, he has never been averse to digging in the trenches of research and ferreting out stories that have been long buried in the traditions and superstitions of everyday folk. Such is the way the lore of those folks–folklore–is retrieved and recorded.

Dr. Ellis has occasionally tapped the memories and research skills of his own students to capture some of the stories within commuting distance of the PSU Hazleton campus. He suggested that they, in turn, interview a friend or relative who might have knowledge about haunted places, ghosts, and the unexplainable.

He was kind enough to share several of the

resultant reports with me, with the proviso that the names of the students not be published.

J.Z., of Drums, as I will identify him, interviewed an aunt who told him he would be happy to tell him some old family tales.

One dated back to the childhood of the woman's father, in about 1900.

Her father and her grandfather, a butcher, were delivering meat on a horse-drawn buckboard from Hazleton to Dorrance. The elder man liked to stop at taverns along the way, and by the time they came to the foot of the Dorrance Mountain, he was in no shape to drive. He handed the reins over to the young lad and took a nap in the buckboard.

As the youngster was urging the horses up the hill, they stopped, reared up, and whinnied frantically. Miffed by their sudden fit of fear, the boy tried his best to calm them.

At once, what the boy described as a white dog, bigger than the horses, emerged from the woods. Without incident, the colossal canine crossed their path. As it disappeared into a stand of trees, the horses quieted down and the boy regained control of them.

According to J.Z.'s aunt, her father swore it was all true and told her that others in the area had told him they saw the same mysterious figure at that same stretch of road. All who crossed paths with the beast believed it to be from another dimension–a ghost.

Her father also told her of the ghostly Indian maiden he once encountered while he was walking from his home in Dorrance into Hazleton. He told her the spirit simply appeared as if from nowhere, strolled silently beside him for a spell, and vanished.

From D.K., also of Drums, came a story his father had told the family about Grape Run (or, as they called it, "Grapy"). It was a coal road near Crystal Ridge and it was said to have been inhabited by a strange force or being. The report writer said her father would never disclose the details of what happened or happens on "Grapy," but he insisted that they stay away from the road... "or else!"

Crystal Ridge was the setting for another story collected by D.K. That one involved her uncle Frank, who was walking home along a desolate dirt road that passed by an old mine shaft.

The only home that ever stood along the road had burned to the ground years ago. It was said that when it burned, several thousands of dollars went up in smoke–money that had been stashed in the walls of the house by its owner.

One moonless night, Frank was walking alone on the road. Even in broad daylight, it was a spooky place. In the pitch blackness of night, it was that much more foreboding.

As he passed the spot where the house once stood, Frank heard the faint sound of what he described as the rattling of chains. Quickly, the sound intensified. And, to his shock, a bright light shone on the site of the fire-ravaged house. Try as he did to determine the source of the sound and the light, he could not. In an instant, the light was snuffed and the rattling ceased.

Frank's leisurely pace turned into a nervous trot as he headed home. He told his story to his wife and grandmother, and both later swore that as he tried to explain what had happened, every visible hair on his body was standing on end.

As Dr. Ellis has been doing for several decades, and as this writer has been doing for 35 years, the collecting of ghost stories, legends, and folklore is a noble and necessary pursuit.

Devoid of legends and lore that spin outside that box we call history, societies would not be much fun.

What previous generations called "tall tales" we now call "urban legends." Perhaps they are not exactly alike, but notions of frightening roads, mysterious creatures, and dark and stormy nights have always been–and *should* always be–the kindling for a tingling.

While many of the stories remain locked in

the imaginations of storytellers and never make it to print, many others have been recorded for all to read and repeat.

While researching this book, I was fascinated by a passage in Stewart Pearce's wonderful 1860 book *Annals of Luzerne County: A Record of Interesting Events, Traditions, and Anecdotes.*

In his chapter on witches, Pearce offered some observations that are as true in the 21st century as they were in the mid-19th century.

"We may laugh at the follies of a past age, and congratulate ourselves on the superior intelligence and condition of our own; but observation will show us that every age has its absurdities and superstitions. The credulity of the first settlers in regard to witches, is equaled by the weakness of multitudes at this day, who cannot pass a graveyard by night without trembling for fear they shall see a spook or ghost.

"The witches of those days scratched upon the walls; the spirits of the 19th century rap on the tables."

Mr. Pearce, if you're out there, know that the spirits of the 21st century show up as orbs on digital pictures and as passages on the Internet.

Oh yes, and as stories in books.

Thankfully, some things haven't changed at all.

It is wonderful that five thousand years have now elapsed since the creation of the world, and still it is undecided whether or not there has ever been an instance of the spirit of any person appearing after death. All argument is against it; but all belief is for it.

Samuel Johnson

Part Three
LORE

THE CARBONDALE UFO INCIDENT:

PENNSYLVANIA'S ROSWELL?

The story was potentially shocking! The "breaking news" on November 10, 1974 was that an unidentified flying object had either crashed or had been shot down from the sky over Salem Mountain, near Carbondale, Pennsylvania. Whatever it was, the UFO wound up in a silt pond near the old DeAngeles Colliery.

For many tense hours, the world waited to hear more details about the story that could have rewritten everything we assumed about the universe. We were not alone.

The incident, reported at 1:30 in the morning, was reported by teenagers who had been "hanging around" the Russell Park area and claimed that they witnessed a fiery, sizzling, yellow-white object with a tail of red sparks soar from out of nowhere and into the pond. It was described as about three times bigger than a basketball, and emitting a gaseous, noxious odor.

Upon arrival, police and emergency units from Carbondale placed the Russell Park area in a lockdown. They sent for the nearest Geiger Counter, contacted the federal UFO information center, and cautiously proceeded to attempt to retrieve the item from the pond. The Civil Air Patrol was called in to stand guard.

As they probed the shallow, murky water with grappling hooks, rumors began to run rampant beyond the perimeter of the scene of the incident.

Were earlier reports of a strange aircraft hovering over the mountain, park, and pond true? Was the area cordoned off because federal authorities were called in? Did those "Feds" indeed find and spirit away the UFO under the cloak of darkness? Did, indeed, those "Feds" *shoot down the craft?*

Word leaked out that there really was a mysterious, glowing object in the water. But, it was proving difficult to retrieve and identify. Rumor had it that a Carbondale police officer actually shot at the item.

Yes, the Carbondale UFO incident was big news in November, 1974. For a couple of days, that is.

On Tuesday, November 12, a news conference in Carbondale revealed that it was all a somewhat elaborate hoax.

The mysterious, glowing object–the alleged UFO–was a lighted lantern tossed into the silt pond by adventurous teenagers who supposedly conspired to call in the initial reports of something odd "hovering" over the hills and something even more odd splashing into the pond.

Not everyone was convinced that the authorities' claim of "hoax" was on the up-and-up.

Some people believed *that* story was concocted to divert attention from the truth: That a UFO actually did crash–*or was shot down*–near Carbondale and the government planted the lantern in the pond.

So, more than three decades later, how does the story play in retrospect?

Stanton T. Friedman, nuclear physicist and one of the most energetic and respected investigators of UFOs in the world, provided this comment about the Carbondale UFO incident, exclusively for this book:

"The case of a supposed crash of a UFO through the ice on a pond in Carbondale, Pennsylvania, in November, 1974, received a lot of attention at the time.

"A number of investigators came by, mostly because it was felt that there was still something under the water.

"Three boys told a story of a mysterious object going in. One has fully confessed that the testimony of the boys was a hoax.

"Some people in the area have recently tried to make a very big deal in the hope of making Carbondale sort of an 'East Coast Roswell,' drawing tourists to a museum of some sort. The diver who retrieved the lantern from underwater has made clear there was nothing special there.

"As the original civilian investigator of the Roswell Incident beginning in the 1970s, I would say there is no comparison at all. I agree with the original investigators and the recent work of Rick Fisher and Matt Graeber that there is much less there than the enthusiasts would have us believe."

UFOlogist Matt Graeber has called the matter "The Carbondale UFO Capers" and, eloquently, "a gleaming facet of contemporary UFOlogical folklore."

Another individual who has taken an interest and made an in-depth study of the Carbondale tale is Rick Fisher, the Lancaster County-based founder of the Paranormal Society of Pennsylvania.

In a statement prepared especially for this book, Fisher assessed the lore and legacy of the 1974 incident:

"I can't really say what happened in Carbondale.

"I have been investigating this for several years. It supposedly was a lantern that caused the three day sensation, but my belief is that it wasn't.

"There are three theories as to what happened–one that it was a lantern, two that it was something from the Soviet Union, or that it was extraterrestrial.

"I don't believe it was lantern, although as of now I have no proof it was something else.

"I have talked to the police who were involved at that time and all believe it was a lantern. I have talked with the teens who were the ones who originally reported the incident. One is deceased, another one claims that he saw something come out of the sky and land in the pond, and the third witness told me he threw the lantern in but believes something else was in the pond.

"Many of the residents don't believe a lantern can stay under water for the three days in question but I did my own test in similar conditions and it stayed lit for 84 hours, but it still doesn't mean it was a lantern.

"I talked to one so called witness and have him on video tape saying he wasn't there until the day they pulled it out and couldn't see much because of all the people who were present. He told someone else he was there the night it happened and saw everything. When I exposed him, he trashed me all over the Internet, even suggesting that I was part of the cover-up.

"So, the real conspiracy may lie with a few individuals who want so bad to believe it was a UFO."

Has the episode that was so hot in 1974 been relegated to the UFO cold case file?

Not according to Rick Fisher, who remains interested and doggedly determined to close the file, at least to his satisfaction.

"I still have a long way to go if this case will ever be solved," he said.

"I have filed under the Freedom of Information Act with various governmental agencies for information and that could take years to get back.

"I am still actively investigating and hope to interview more witnesses who were present. It's interesting and I hope I am able to crack the case someday."

The case is certainly not "cold," if its presence on the Internet is any indication. The debate about the incident and its interpretations continues to simmer on the web, and is likely to never cool down.

FROM
THE HALE-BOPP
COMET COMES THE
GREATEST AND THE MOST
INCREDIBLE NEWS EVENT AND
MYSTERY IN THE HISTORY OF THE
WORLD! IT IS THE GREATEST STORY
IN WORLD HISTORY, CENSORED BY THE
ESTABLISHMENT. THE STORY THEY DO NOT
WANT YOU TO KNOW!....KNOWLEDGE FROM
ANOTHER WORLD!...WE PROUDLY PRESENT TO YOU

THE SECRET OF OLYPHANT!

For years, John J. Peruka has waged a mostly one-man campaign to prove that, in simple terms, his adopted hometown of Olyphant is the center of the known universe.

"The whole theory," he said, "is based on the revolutionary concept that everything in the universe–and I mean everything from the lowly quarks and electrons of the atom to the giant galaxies–are made from 'pyramids of light.'

"There are too many objects in nature which resemble triangles, but they are distorted and you have to use your imagination to see them. And, a triangle is related to a pyramid. Remember that this is an abstract mathematical idea and the perfect pyramid exists in Plato's pure geometrical forms and is mathematically abstract."

With that as a preamble, Peruka continued to present his case that Olyphant is the result of a deep, mysterious mathematical and paranormal creation.

That, of course, is a pitifully inadequate summation of Peruka's work. The dossier he provided for this chapter in this book totaled more than 160 pages.

"The town of Olyphant," he said, "has an incredible hidden world that no one knew about. They didn't see any pictures of the Great Pyramid and Sphinx for about two years until they were posted on the Internet.

"This is very important because it turns a very interesting story into the greatest story of all time!"

Peruka admitted he has been ridiculed by some townsfolk and bloggers on the web. But, he has continued to push his theories nonetheless.

"The people of Olyphant built Olyphant, but they did not create it," he asserted. "A supernatural force controlled their minds and they didn't know it. This is the most important part of the theory and many researchers and scientists missed this point: Who Created Olyphant?"

Peruska said many researchers have studied the theory, but most have rejected it.

"They have censored it," he said. "For every claim that I make I provide sufficient evidence."

Indeed he does–all 160 pages of it.

Peruska does go out on a limb–several limbs, and some thinner than others–with some of his assertions. Among the quotes from his work:

℘ *"The spirit of Houdini resides all over Olyphant."*

℘ *"Olyphant is a doorway into another world, a door to God."*

℘ *"Discovered in Olyphant: A Sphinx five miles long and the location of the Holy Grail."*

℘ *"Even towns have secrets. The town of Olyphant has a secret so terrifying that it could change the course of world history."*

He calls Olyphant "a town of incredible magic and mystery," and cites some interesting findings that he has made regarding the layout, landmarks, and of the town and how they support his theories:

ΔWhen traced, the boundaries of the town resemble a Sphinx. (It does, sort of)

ΔWhen traced, the Christian churches of town form the shape of the constellation Orion, with the Jewish temple in the middle. (They do, sort of)

ΔOlyphant is 960 feet above sea level. That is exactly double the height of the Great Pyramid. (Yes, and so?)

ΔA long-eroded culm dump between Olyphant and Throop was once the perfect shape of a Pyramid.

ΔThe blades of the landmark anchor (of the aircraft carrier USS Wasp) at Blakely Corners

represent the wings of a Phoenix bird and have
been used by extraterrestrials for navigation.
ΔThe UFO discussed in the previous story was
actually soaring from outer space and heading for
the "door" in Olyphant when it went out of control
and crashed into the silt pond at Russell Park.
(Even Peruska admitted that was just speculation
and needs much more research)

The anchor of the USS Wasp, at Blakely Corners.

Is John Peruska on to something?

He has meticulously and tirelessly gathered information from biblical, metaphysical, celestial, historical, and geographical sources and has wound and weaved that information around the curious findings he has made about Olyphant.

I found Olyphant to be a hospitable town with friendly people and absolutely amazing architectural gems. Do those people stand on the portal of something that could indeed rewrite the history of the universe as we know it?

Has John Peruska found the keys and is he opening locks that should have remained sealed forever?

Peruska's work and his seemingly ludicrous theories warrant closer examination (and, they're all over the Internet–do a search) if only for his intensity and sincerity. He truly believes that yes, he is on to something.

"Many scientists and researchers throughout the world have studied this theory and said that it was revolutionary, profound, extremely interesting, ingenious, very exciting, and provocative," he said. "But, because of its extraordinary claims, they have censored it."

...and more!

COAL COUNTRY GHOSTS
LEGENDS & LORE
BOOK TWO
More tales from Schuylkill & Carbon counties
COMING SOON!
FROM EXETER HOUSE BOOKS

ABOUT THE AUTHOR

Charles J. Adams III was born in Reading, Pennsylvania, in 1947 and resides there today. In addition to his books, Adams also writes regular features on travel and local legends in the *Reading Eagle* newspaper. In addition, he is the morning air personality on radio station WEEU in Reading.

Adams has been a speaker at many paranormal conferences and has been interviewed on ghostly topics in England, Ireland, South Africa, and on several American radio and television stations. He has also appeared on The History Channel and has served as consultant and on-air "expert" for programs on hauntings and ghosts on The Learning Channel, MTV, and The Travel Channel.

Adams has also organized and escorted tours of haunted places in the United States, England, and Scotland.

He has produced, written, and conducted "ghost tours" in Lancaster County, Reading, and Philadelphia, Pa.; Cape May, N.J., and Greenwich Village, New York City. His stories have been selected for inclusion in several anthologies. Charlie has also served as president of the Reading (Pa.) Public Library, the Board of Directors of the Exeter Township School District, and on the boards of the Penn State Berks Campus Alumni Society, Exeter Community Library, and the Historical Society of Berks County. In 2006, Adams organized the inaugural "READING READS: The Greater Reading Literary Festival." He also donated a personal collection of nearly 400 books about ghosts, legends, and folklore from around the world to the Exeter Community Library as "The Charles J. Adams III Paranormal Research Collection."